## PRAISE FOR RESCUE YOUR DREAMS

**Honestly, this doesn't feel like a self-help book at all, which is precisely why it's so impactful.** While full of facts and structured advice, it feels more like a conversation with a friend who is gently, but directly, guiding you forward on a path that works.

*Rescue Your Dreams* was easy to read but... hard to put down to do the suggested exercises! I simply wanted to know what thought-provoking question Adam would offer next.

**To say I recommend this book is an understatement. I wish I had it years ago; it would have saved me a lot of work and heartache.**

— **Sheila McCraith**
Author of *Yell Less, Love More*
Creator of The Orange Rhino Challenge®

---

**Adam doesn't talk *at* you. He talks *to* you—with heart and clarity, and it lights a fire under your ass.**

This book isn't filled with fluffy rah-rah nonsense or recycled Pinterest quotes. It's packed with real, actionable advice and challenges that make you stop, reflect, and—most importantly—move.

Even when I thought, "I've heard this before," Adam found a way to flip it and help me see new ways forward.

**If you feel stuck, if your dreams are buried under excuses and fear—grab this book.**

— **Tom Reber**
Founder of The Contractor Fight®
Business Coach

**Here's the thing about Adam Mock: He won't let you drift. He won't let you settle. He won't let you keep telling yourself the same tired story about why your dreams can wait.**

I've known Adam for nearly two decades, and I've seen him do what he does best—ignite people's potential, encourage their hearts, and remind them that playing small was never the plan.

And now, he's done it in a book.

*Rescue Your Dreams* **isn't just words on a page; it's a permission slip to remember what you really want and a battle plan to go get it.**

Read it. Sit with it. Let it do its work.

**- Scott Hodge**
Founder & Lead Curator, Society 57

---

**Having the wisdom of Adam Mock in your pocket is an incredible asset—one that has the power to pour rocket fuel on the areas of life that feel stalled out, dried out, or out of alignment.**

Like potent medicine for a life that's lost its pulse, *Rescue Your Dreams* gives you the tools to dismantle the false narratives that keep you anchored in place. **Adam doesn't just illuminate the path forward... he hands you the map to walk it boldly.**

This book will challenge you, shake you, and, if you let it, transform you.

**- Benjamin Jay Thomas**
Singer/Songwriter
Transformational Creativity Coach

**I love the tough love approach Adam has.** There's a gentle nudge followed by a stern talking-to that gives us the accountability check we all need while still providing a safe space for growth.

He is real in how he coaches. It's okay to be afraid—we grow there. It's okay to stumble—we are stronger when we stand up.

**This guidebook provides a genius blueprint for leaders and learners of all levels to rescue the life you thought was lost!**

**- Staci Boyer**
Author of *Motiv8n'U*
IFBB Pro
Navy Veteran, VFW Commander

---

***Rescue Your Dreams* is a book that will wake you up.** Adam has created a not-so-subtle framework to remind us of the visions and aspirations that have been covered by obligations, fears, failures, and doubts.

To discover the incredible hope Adam writes into the invitation that is within these pages, you will need to not only be honest, do the homework, but also somewhere in the process you will have the opportunity to believe again.

**And that is what is available in the lines and chapters: the opportunity and framework to believe again—and to rescue your dreams.**

And that is everything.

**- Hendre Coetzee**
Leadership Architect
C-Suite Coach

*Rescue Your Dreams* is a practical and heartfelt guide to help you remember what you really want.

Adam's real-life examples and experiences will help you uncover what's been holding you back from your dream life. His words are impactful and real. It isn't always easy to dig deep and get honest with yourself, but Adam will help you navigate it with purpose and passion.

**With his help, you truly can rescue your dreams and save the life you forgot you wanted.**

- **Tammy Helfrich**
Intuitive Life Coach
Author of *Unapologetic* and *Ablaze*

**The time spent with you was more valuable than all the trainings I've attended over the past 8 years combined.** To say I'm grateful is an understatement.

**It always amazes me how you can *see* me and my experiences so clearly.** You are very good at what you do, and I am so very grateful for all your wisdom, insight, and guidance. **You WOW me!!!!**

Can I just tell you, **you're a guru ROCKSTAR!!!** Earlier today, I used the method you taught me with someone I know very well . . . **GAME CHANGER!!!!**

I cannot wait to set up another session with you soon. LOVE THEM! I get so much from these sessions. First, I can ask some very specific questions. Second, we end up talking, getting on some tangents and **you drop these knowledge bombs that have been so relevant it's scary.**

Thank you so much for sharing your time, your energy, and your wisdom. **I am continuously blown away by your ability to communicate complex ideas in a way that people can relate to and make actionable.**

**You have no idea the powerful impact you've made on my life.** You helped me find my voice and gave me my first real vehicle to show the world what I was made of!

Thank you again for an incredible coaching session, **I walked away feeling lighter and more hopeful than I have in a very long time.**

*Read more at: adammock.com*

# RESCUE
# YOUR
# DREAMS

## A GUIDEBOOK TO SAVE THE LIFE YOU FORGOT YOU WANTED

# ADAM MOCK, LCS
## FOREWORD: DOUG MCKINLEY, PSY.D.

Published by Rescue Your Dreams® Media
Aliso Viejo, CA

Published by Rescue Your Dreams® Media
First Edition
Library of Congress Control Number: 2025904224

ISBN (Paperback): 979-8-9925595-0-7
ISBN (eBook - EPUB): 979-8-9925595-1-4
ISBN (Audio): 979-8-9925595-2-1

This book is intended for informational and educational purposes only. While it provides professional insights and strategies, it is not a substitute for personalized advice, coaching, counseling, therapy, or professional consultation. The author and publisher assume no responsibility for how the information in this book is applied. Readers are encouraged to seek professional guidance when necessary.

For more information on how you can Rescue Your Dreams® or connect with Adam Mock, LCS, please visit: **ADAMMOCK.COM**

*Dedicated to all the dreamers.*
*Go boldly, ever upward.*

# ACKNOWLEDGMENTS

**Deanna Davisson**, your friendship saved my life. I wouldn't be here if you hadn't answered your phone that night. Your presence in that moment changed everything, and I'm forever grateful for your light when I was in such darkness.

**Doug McKinley**, your kindness, generosity, and wisdom have been a guiding presence in my life. One lunch at the airport with you sparked a transformation that became the foundation for this book. Thank you for being such a warm and brilliant force of encouragement.

**Caleb Luper**, you consistently model how to live with passion and purpose. Thank you for being a friend of such high character and for showing me how to elevate others. This world moves forward in great ways because of you.

**Melissa Umali**, thank you for always laughing at my nonsense (even when it involves vending machines). Your calm presence in the storm is a rare and priceless gift, and I'm incredibly grateful for your friendship and to be doing this work with you.

**My friends**, whether you have journeyed with me for a season or are walking with me for this lifetime, you have shaped who I am in ways you may never know. Thank you for being part of the adventure.

**My clients**, thank you for keeping me sharp. Your courage to do the hard work for meaningful change proves that it's never too late to rescue your dreams and transform your reality. You make my heart smile.

**My daughter Magpie**, my kiddo, you make me so proud. Your commitment to learning timeless wisdom and ancient truths is already helping others uncover the best parts of themselves. Keep lighting the way forward!

**My son Gabriel**, my buddy, I'm equally proud of you. Your ability to dive deep into life's complexities has made you an incredible thought leader at a young age. Your care for others has been nothing short of lifesaving.

**My wife Sara**, my Pal, thank you for always believing in me and being my biggest fan. In a world that pressures us to wear masks to fit in, you've always seen me for who I truly am and celebrated it. Your laughter and smile are infectious, and your desire to see a world that plays, creates, and heals is inspiring. Thank you for showing me how vibrant and beautiful life can be.

**And to those in a season of darkness**, remember—it's only 4:00 a.m., and the sun hasn't risen yet.

# CONTENTS

Foreword 1

How To Use This Guidebook 3

Introduction 7

You Are Here. You Want To Be There. 11

Part 1: Who Are You? 17

    Chapter 1: We're All Liars 21

    Chapter 2: The Best Policy 49

    Chapter 3: Stand and Deliver 71

Part 2: Where Are You Going? 95

    Chapter 4: Mapping The Path 101

    Chapter 5: Unmet Needs are Derailers 117

    Chapter 6: The Power of Connection 135

    Chapter 7: Weeds and Walls 157

    Chapter 8: Your Wings Aren't Made of Fear 179

Part 3: Why Are You Going There? 201

    Chapter 9: What's the Point of Purpose 207

    Chapter 10: How Bad Do You Want It? 221

Ever Upward 243

# FOREWORD

As a psychotherapist and leadership consultant these past 30+ years, I have been fascinated by the gap between what people say they believe and what they actually do. The view individuals hold of themselves, in part, shapes the lives they ultimately live—their likes and dislikes, values and beliefs, and of course, their dreams and aspirations.

Some people dare not dream lest they become disappointed with the reality that those dreams may not come true. Others dream big and then become discouraged by the vast competition and often persecution they receive for the very things they want to create.

I have spent my career encouraging people to explore that authentic voice inside themselves—the voice that calls them forward into the life they always wanted to live.

A while back, I was discussing this topic with a young man who clearly had a lot going for himself yet lived a very secure life where others were providing direction and safe harbor for his dreams. He was grateful for his life but never really felt released to go for more.

Through a series of serendipitous conversations with him, possibilities began lifting the veil of complacency as seeds were planted in a receptive mind of curiosity and creativity.

This was Adam Mock.

This cleverly written book was inspired by that awakened mind, shaped by some of the very tools Adam will share with you in these pages. After reading the manuscript, I found it to be a personal and self-directed coaching manual for people who are tired of believing lies about themselves that clearly are not true.

Adam writes like he speaks—direct and to the point.

If you prefer dancing around your personal cliffs of comparisons or allowing head trash to continue living in your mind rent-free, this book may not be for you.

However, if you want to be shaken out of your complacency and fears, if you're ready to unlock your long-hidden dreams, you have found the right guide.

With his own experience and expertise, Adam will lead you in understanding your mindset and what it will take to rescue those dreams that are right within your reach.

I endorse this book wholeheartedly.

I've witnessed Adam come alive over the past several years and am thrilled he chose to engage in the painstaking process of crafting a way to share it with you.

My recommendation is to read, contemplate, and then act on what you discover to be true.

You will be glad you did.

**- Doug McKinley, Psy.D.**
Author of *The Resiliency Quest*
Host of *The Leadership Currency Podcast*

# HOW TO USE THIS GUIDEBOOK

This book is your guide to saving the life you forgot you wanted—the one buried beneath doubts, expectations, comparisons, distractions, and all the crap life throws at you.

I've committed to bringing my authentic voice to these pages so that you can find yours. Which means I'm not trying to be clever with my words.

I'm just being me.

And in order for you to Rescue Your Dreams, you need to do the same. So, commit to being honest with yourself as you proceed through these pages.

It might get uncomfortable.

It might even hurt.

But I promise that it won't kill you.

This journey is a slow, deliberate walk, into the heart of who you really are. So please, take your time and keep at it. I've even purposely spaced out the visuals of this book to be easier to digest and absorb—reminding you to moderate your pace.

Each section is designed to make you think, reflect, and dig deep. And it won't always be easy—real growth never is. It takes six months on average for meaningful change, which means you need to be committed to consistently—not perfectly—doing the work necessary to rescue your dreams.

The way this guidebook works is simple and transformative: it's divided into three major parts that asks you powerful, life changing questions:

- **Who are you?**
- **Where are you going?**
- **Why are you going there?**

Your responses to these questions will be the compass that guides your life. Answer them truthfully, and you'll never feel lost again.

Each chapter is designed to be a steppingstone, leading you through the dark wilderness of your doubts and fears toward the life you truly want. Some topics will resurface in later chapters and build upon what you know and have learned.

Along the way there will be exercises and questions that you must engage in before moving on. And they're intentionally woven into the fabric of each chapter, much like having a conversation with a good friend.

Life itself doesn't wait until the perfect moment to present its challenges, and because of that, you shouldn't wait to take action when prompted.

Too often, we put off doing the work we need to, for the life we want. But this guidebook encourages you to dive in right when asked to—even if it's inconvenient. When you hit an exercise or activity, get up and do it. Let it disrupt your flow. Let it force you to pause and engage, because rescuing your dreams is worth the interruption.

Don't assume an exercise doesn't apply to where you are in life. It's easy to dismiss things as not pertinent to what you're going through and skip ahead to the parts that you *think* are more relevant.

But don't fool yourself.

Every exercise you engage with becomes a new tool in your arsenal—or at least a sharper one. Keep them ready and polished so you can reach for them when the storms of life press on you.

Let each idea sink in, challenge your limiting beliefs, and rewrite your story with every chapter. Meaning, don't just read it—live it. We're not aiming for surface-level change; we're going for transformation that sticks. Absorb the lessons, allow them to reshape your mindset, and deeply integrate them into your life.

The biggest mistake you can make with this guidebook is rushing through it.

So, pause when you need to.

Reflect.

Let yourself sit with the hard questions.

It's okay to take a few days—or even longer—with some parts of this book. Just don't let this guidebook gather dust, because that's how dreams get buried.

Remember, this is your journey—a journey to rescue the life you forgot you wanted. So, take your time, free yourself from distractions, and commit to this process.

Now, here's your first assignment: grab a fresh journal or notebook that you can dedicate to this journey—and don't move ahead until you have it.

Then, open to its first page and in the middle of it write:

**I'm committed to doing the work necessary for meaningful change in my life!**

Now, let's go rescue your dreams.

"Get busy with life's purpose, toss aside empty hopes, get active in your own rescue—if you care for yourself at all—and do it while you can."

- *Marcus Aurelius*

When did you stop dreaming of the life you truly wanted?

I bet it didn't happen all at once. Maybe it was when life got busy, and you started accepting other people's expectations for your life instead of your own. Maybe it was the day you settled for "good enough" because striving for something more seemed too far away. Or maybe it was when a lack of self-confidence started whispering that your dreams were unrealistic.

However it happened, just because you stopped dreaming doesn't mean your dreams died.

They're still there, buried under doubts, expectations, and anxiety, waiting for you to rescue them.

That's why I wrote this book. Because so many dreams are suffocating under the weight of insecurity, fear, and all the ways we "should" on ourselves. And we urgently need to (re)discover where they are.

But the world wants you to believe that dreams are something you chase.

That's ridiculous.

The life you want more than anything else isn't running away from you, playing hard to get. It wants to be embraced, but it's buried. Drowning. Held captive by lies. And it desperately needs rescuing.

If we spend our time believing that we have to constantly pursue the life that we want, we'll never slow down long enough to realize that what we're "chasing" is already within us.

This book is about one thing: rescuing the life you forgot you wanted. The life that still pulses with possibility, no matter how deeply buried it feels right now.

I know this because I've been there.

On April 10, 1996, I decided to end my life.

I was 23, lost in darkness. My dreams weren't just buried—they were dead. Or at least that's how it felt. Months of numbing the pain with pills, alcohol, and over-the-counter meds left me empty and hopeless. I couldn't see a way forward. I didn't even believe there was one.

That night, I picked up two razor blades—one for each wrist. I wrote a goodbye note and resolved that this would be my last day alive.

But before I went through with it, I made one phone call to a friend. She didn't try to fix me or give me a speech. But through her fear and pleading she asked me one simple question:

"Adam, can you give me one more day?"

I don't know why, but I agreed. Maybe because the request was small enough to feel doable. Maybe because I thought I could always go through with it tomorrow if nothing changed. Either way, I said yes.

And that's when *everything* changed.

On April 11, 1996, I woke up.

Really woke up.

By some divine intervention the darkness that had clouded my life lifted. For the first time in what felt like forever, I could see color. I had an immense spiritual awakening that changed how I saw the world. It wasn't just a shadow anymore.

It was alive.

Looking back, I realize I had no idea how far my life was from what I truly wanted. There was this massive chasm between my reality and the life I'd dreamed of for myself. Bridging that gap seemed impossible back then, but I'm here to tell you it's not only possible—it's necessary.

So, let's get rid of this notion that you need to chase your dreams—they aren't running away from you. But if you picked up this book, they need rescuing. And this guide is here to show you how to set them free.

And if you ever feel like the work is too hard, that you're too old, too far gone, or too tired, give yourself a gift:

One more day.

One more day to try, strive, build, reclaim, get up, and imperfectly move yourself ahead.

Let's start by taking the first step, getting honest about where you are today—because you can't rescue your dreams unless you first acknowledge the gap.

# YOU ARE HERE.
# YOU WANT TO BE THERE.

Grab your journal and open to the next blank page. At the top of the page write: **I am here.**

We're starting with your current reality.

I want you to be brutally honest. Not the masked version you might show the world, but the raw, unfiltered truth of where you are right now. I'm talking about the stuff you feel and ruminate on when no one's watching.

Think about your average day. The good, the bad, the things that make you smile, and the things you'd rather keep hidden.

I want you to write down what an average day in your life looks and feels like. We all fall into patterns so if you're not happy with where you are it's vital that you assess what's not working for you.

Start with how things are when you wake up in the morning. Your first thought and your priorities. Then continue to move through your average day filling in the afternoon and evening, culminating with when you go to bed.

Here's some questions to help guide you:

- **Where are you, right now, in your life?**

  What does your everyday environment look and feel like? Not just at home, but work too, and the places you regularly visit. Even down to the inside of your car that you're using for your commutes.

  What do think about yourself? Do you dread looking in the mirror? Do you feel that you have value, or do you feel worthless? How's your health? Are you making the most of your physical abilities or are you allowing them to slowly fade away?

Are you happy with where you are or frustrated that things will never change?

- **Who's around you—who are the people in your space?**

  If you're in a relationship, does it feel habitual or like it's growing in a healthy direction? Do wish you could find a way out of it, or a way to have a richer and deeper sense of intimacy?

  What's your friend circle like? Do you have one? Are you alone? Do your friends encourage, inspire, and challenge you to be your best? Or do they complain, drag you down, and don't want you to do better than them?

  How about family? Are you married? Kids? Pets? Are you a caregiver to aging parents? Do you have a good or strained relationship with your siblings?

- **What do you do with your time, day in and day out?**

  Do you have a job? Does it feel meaningful, or does it just pay the bills?

  When you have free time what do you choose to do? Explore new things? Learn? Binge your favorite shows? Numb with alcohol or drugs? Sleep? Hang with friends or family?

  Do you have a hobby? Does that hobby give you a sense of community or do you use it to isolate? Are you pursuing your interests or saying to yourself, "One day I will …"?

- **How does your average day make you feel, deep down?**

  Be as descriptive as possible. How do you really feel when you wake up? How do you feel as you move through your day? Do you feel angry? Sad? Frustrated? Bored? Scared? Anxious? Depressed? Content? Stressed?

  What do those feelings lead to?Shutting down? Opening up? Hiding? Avoiding? Numbing? Seeking?

  What thoughts do you have about the world around you? Do you feel safe? Seen? Valued? Do feel that you have to do it all alone? Or do you feel that you're connected?

Don't hold back. The more honest you are, the clearer the picture becomes.

When you're done, take a minute to read through it. And take heart, this current life of yours will become more meaningful, intentional, and purposeful by the time you're done with this book.

Now, open to the next blank page in your journal and at the top write: **I want to be here.**

Take a breath and let yourself dream. Picture the life you've always wanted but may have never thought was possible. The one that lights you up, that makes you excited to wake up in the morning.

The life where you're exactly where you're meant to be.

Now start writing out what an average day in your dream life looks and feels like. Just like before, start with when you wake up. Look back up at the previous questions with this new lens and see how your answers change. And don't hold back.

Here is another framework that may help you:

- **What does that dream life look like in vivid detail?**

- **Where are you living it?**

- **Who are the people you've surrounded yourself with?**

- **What are you doing that makes you feel alive, with purpose and joy?**

Did you feel that shift in your spirit when you wrote about your dream life versus your current reality?

Good.

That feeling is your compass. Write down every detail. Let yourself get lost in the vision of the life you deserve.

---

## THE GAP

---

Now, take a good, hard look at what you've written. Compare your current life with your dream life, side by side. That space in between them—that's your gap. That's the distance between where you are and where you want to be.

That's how deep your dreams have been buried.

It may be uncomfortable to face, but this is the moment where your transformation begins. That gap is your guide. It's the spotlight that shows you how far you've held yourself back—the limiting beliefs and the self-doubt that have kept you stuck.

But now it's time to set your intention: to commit to closing that gap.

Flip back to the first page of your journal and read what you wrote out loud:

**I'm committed to doing the work necessary for meaningful change in my life!**

This is your promise. The decision to stop drifting and start taking control. The gap between you and your dream life will get smaller with every move you make, as long as you keep showing up for yourself.

With each chapter, you'll chip away at the barriers that have been blocking your way. The more you dig in, the more you'll see that the distance between where you are and where you want to be isn't as massive as you thought.

Progress might be slow at first, but every step forward builds momentum.

So remember:

No rushing.

No skipping ahead.

And no downplaying your feelings.

As you work through this guidebook, come back to these reflections whenever you need a reality check. Remember where you started and recognize how far you've come. This is your journey to rescue the life you forgot you wanted, and it's not just a destination—it's a commitment to living fully, every single day.

Now, it's time to dive into Part 1.

**I'm looking forward to meeting the person
you're meant to be.**

# PART 1
## WHO ARE YOU?

# WHO ARE YOU?

The most important conversation you'll ever have—is the one with yourself.

To make that conversation a healthy one, you need to truly know who you are. Not your job title, the roles you play, or the labels society has given you. I'm talking about the version of you that isn't performing for others—the raw, unfiltered you that shows up when no one's watching.

This section is about excavating that true self. Over the next three chapters, we'll strip away what's holding you back: the fears, doubts, and mental clutter keeping you from seeing yourself clearly. You'll discover what's real and what's just head trash.

Because the truth is, if you don't know who you are, you'll never really know where you're going. Your choices will always be shaped by what others want for you, what society expects from you, or even what you think you should want. Instead of living a life that's authentically yours, you'll be sailing by someone else's stars.

But this work takes courage and honesty—qualities you already have if you've picked up this book.

We'll clear out the mental narratives that don't serve you, take an honest look at your strengths and weaknesses, and help you stand and deliver to the world a clearer sense of who you are.

We're not searching for perfection here—perfection is an illusion. Instead we're uncovering the truth. Even if it's messy, raw, and not what you expected. Because when you do, you'll finally be able to answer the question that most people avoid:

Who are you?

# CHAPTER 1

## WE'RE ALL LIARS

We all have that inner critic that loves to crash the party, don't we? The one who never gets an invite but somehow always shows up.

The one that's way too comfortable pointing out that you're not good enough, you're not smart enough, and doggone it, people don't like you.

That voice has a name—it's called head trash, and it's been living rent-free in your mind for way too long.

And it's time to get rid of the squatter.

Your head trash is also known as "stinkin' thinkin'" and more commonly as limiting beliefs.

But no matter what name you use, these are the sneaky little thoughts that convince you to stay small. They're the invisible chains wrapped around your ambition, whispering, *Don't reach too high, You're not ready,* or *You'll never achieve that.*

These beliefs are like self-imposed ceilings that keep you from even looking at the stars, let alone reaching them.

But those beliefs aren't facts. They're lies.

They're stories you've told yourself, narratives that got stitched together from every doubt, every no, and every setback you've ever experienced.

And although these lies seem like they're set in stone, they're not. And you have the sledgehammer to break through them—you just need to start swinging.

## WHERE THIS STUFF COMES FROM

Most of this head trash didn't even start with you. It's the voice of controlling parents, some not-so-great teachers, and  the loud social media society—telling you who you are and how you should live. And somewhere along the way, you started believing it.

These beliefs sneak into your head, set up shop, and before you know it, they're calling the shots in your life. They tell you what you can and can't do, what you're allowed to want, and how far you're allowed to dream.

But just because those voices are loud doesn't mean they're right.

They're just echoes of someone else's fear, doubt, and limitations that you've been carrying around like your own personal baggage. These aren't your truths—they're someone else's garbage, disguised as your inner dialogue.

We're like sponges. We soak up everything—the good, the bad, and the completely useless. We absorb the fears and doubts of others and make them our own. And once we do, they start to sound real, don't they?

They start to sound like they originate from inside us.

But the reality is, they're just stories—hand-me-down narratives that need to be tossed out or rewritten. Because if you don't, you might just believe those stories are actually who you are.

So, let's take out the trash in your mind first.

Then we'll silence those outer voices.

---

## FLIPPING THE SCRIPT

---

Flipping the script is about taking back control of the stories that have been holding you down. And, reshaping the entire narrative that's been limiting your potential.

This isn't some fake positivity exercise or pretending everything's fine. Because if you're living someone else's lies everything is not fine. What we need to do is challenge those lies and turn them into a mindset that actually serves you.

For example, every time you catch yourself thinking, *I'm not enough*, I want you to hit pause and ask yourself, *Who decided that?* Who said you weren't capable, and why should their voice have more weight than your own?

When you begin to question these beliefs, you'll see they're just echoes of someone else's fear.

And most of these beliefs fall apart when you confront them head-on. They're not facts—they're just someone else's insecurity that you've mistaken for your own truth.

But remember:

**Just because they said it doesn't mean it's true.**

It's so easy to blast through that sentence and move on. Look at it again and really let it sink in. Because if you keep believing those lies, it will affect everything you do.

What you believe, affects how you feel, which affects how you behave.

That's worth saying out loud:

**What I believe, affects how I feel, which affects how I behave.**

So, if you believe you'll never have the life of your dreams, you'll feel that nothing you do will matter, so you'll do just that—nothing.

YOU are the author of your own story, and it's time to start writing one based on your values, your potential, and your truth—not the head trash that's been stinking up your mind.

---

## HOW TO FLIP THE SCRIPT: STEP-BY-STEP

---

### 1. Catch the Thought:

The moment you notice a limiting belief creeping in, stop and say it out loud.

*Yeah, out loud.*

Call it out for what it is—a mental barrier trying to hold you back.

For instance, when you catch yourself thinking, *I'm not good enough,* stop. Then listen to how ridiculous that sounds out loud.

After you say it, I want you to say, *No. That's not true. It's a lie.*

## 2. Reframe and Reclaim:

Now, reframe that thought into something that empowers you and say it out loud.

- **Limiting Belief:** I'm too old to start over.

  **Reframe:** My experience gives me the wisdom and knowledge to ignite the next chapter of my life.

- **Limiting Belief:** I've failed too many times before.

  **Reframe:** Now I know what not to do. I've learned what doesn't work and how to navigate more clearly—let's keep going.

- **Limiting Belief:** I'm not good enough.

  **Reframe:** I'm good enough to start and skill grows with practice. Let's get to work.

## 3. Focus on Momentum:

Shift your focus from what you think is an anchor to a full-blown windsail. Don't ignore the challenges—instead, see them as momentum builders, not roadblocks. Let them become the fuel that keeps you moving forward.

You're not as fragile as you feel.

With each step of consistency, each challenge you overcome, and every doubter you prove wrong, you'll only grow stronger.

Flipping the script is about empowering yourself, acknowledging the obstacles, and choosing to focus on how you'll grow and overcome them instead of getting stuck on the problem.

# THE POWER OF WORDS

Words matter.

Even the ones in your internal dialogue.

They shape how you see yourself, how you approach challenges, and how you show up in the world.

When you flip the script, you're rewiring the way you think. You're training your brain to focus on possibilities instead of limitations, on solutions instead of problems.

The words you use—especially the ones you say to yourself—become the lens through which you see the world. Change your words, and you change your life.

And here's a little self-talk hack: Stop using absolutes like, *always* or *never*.

Replace them with, *sometimes* or *right now*. This small shift opens the door to change. It's your reminder: Where you are today isn't where you have to stay tomorrow.

Think about it: "I always mess things up" shuts down the possibility of growth, while "Sometimes I make mistakes, but I'm learning" leaves room for improvement.

Or consider, "I'll never be good at this." That's a wall that blocks progress. Swap it for "Right now, this is tough, but I can figure it out," and suddenly, you've created space for effort and growth.

These small shifts in language are powerful—they change how you see challenges and how you move forward.

# WHAT YOU DON'T KNOW HAS BEEN HURTING YOU

You can't change what you're not aware of.

Awareness is like turning on the light switch in a dark room—it shows you where the obstacles are, the stuff you've been breaking your pinky toe on, and what you need to move out of your way.

The more you notice those limiting beliefs sneaking into your thoughts, the more power you have to shut them down.

But the trick is to catch these thoughts in the act.

Not after they've already convinced you to back down or give up, but right at the moment they start whispering their filthy little lies. That's how change happens—when you stop letting those beliefs run wild and start kicking them out so you can see the truth.

And please …

Let the door hit 'em in the ass on their way out.

Because when you do that, you become more resilient.

Resilience is about getting back up every single time your limiting beliefs trip you up. It's flexing that mental muscle and getting stronger at shutting down the thoughts that don't serve you.

This is where awareness comes into play.

It's the superpower that allows you to catch yourself in the act of negative thinking before it ruins the show. The more aware you become, the quicker you'll be at spotting those old patterns creeping in.

And every time you do, you get a chance to choose differently.

One of the most effective ways to do this is called **pattern interruption.** It's exactly what it sounds like—a way to disrupt that spiral of negative thinking before it picks up momentum.

**Here's how you do it:** the moment you catch yourself spiraling, do something to physically or mentally snap yourself out of it.

Stand up.

Stretch.

Say it out loud.

Clap your hands if you have to.

It might feel a little ridiculous at first, but that's the point. You're breaking the cycle. You're creating space between the thought and your reaction to it.

You need to reclaim control over your own mind and not let those automatic lies dictate your actions. The more you practice interrupting these patterns, the faster you'll be at stopping them in their tracks.

---

## ACTIONS FOR LONG-TERM MINDSET SHIFTS

---

Changing your mindset isn't just a switch you flip; it's a habit you build. It's like training for a marathon—you don't just lace up your shoes and run 26 miles on day one. You start with one step, then another, and over time, those steps add up.

The same goes for creating a mindset that supports your goals instead of sabotaging them.

The key here is consistency over intensity. Instead of making a massive shift overnight, show up every day and do the work necessary to reframe your thoughts. Turn these new beliefs into your default setting.

To help you get some reps in, I'm laying out three exercises to start clearing out the head trash and make room for a healthier mindset.

One you'll do now.

One you'll do for 30 days.

One you'll do daily as an ongoing new habit.

*I dare you.*

Grab your journal and open to a blank page. At the top, write:

### The beliefs that have been holding me back:

Take a deep breath, and list the three most challenging beliefs you face regularly.

These are the thoughts that creep in when you think about your goals or dreams—the ones that make you hesitate, doubt, or keep you stuck.

Once you've listed them, rank them:

## 1. The Lackey Level

This is the grunt-level belief—the one that's small and easy to handle but still gets in your way. Like the minor enemies in a game, it's there to trip you up, but defeating it is just a warm-up for what's to come.

Clearing this level will give you your first win and set you up for bigger battles ahead.

## 2. The Gatekeeper

Now you're facing a mid-level villain—the belief that feels heavier and more challenging.

This is The Gatekeeper, standing in your way, testing your skills and determination. It's not insurmountable, but it will take focus and consistency to overcome.

Taking it down unlocks the next level.

## 3. The Boss Fight

Here it is—the belief that's been running the show for far too long. This is your endgame: The Boss Fight with its dramatic music, massive health bar, and intimidating presence. It's big, it's bad, but you're ready.

With all the tools and confidence you've gained, you'll walk away victorious—and this belief will never haunt you again.

Got them? Great. Now let's start slaying them, one by one.

---

## DO THIS NOW

---

We're starting with a quick win—something to show yourself that you've got what it takes to shift your mindset. Take the easiest limiting belief you've listed—The Lackey. This is where we'll start.

- **Write It Down:**
  Grab your journal and write this belief at the top of its own page.

- **Say It Out Loud:**
  Speak the belief out loud and really listen to it. Let yourself hear

how ridiculous or false it sounds.

- **After you say it, respond out loud:**
  "No. That's not true. It's a lie."

- **List the Evidence:**
  Write all the reasons this belief *feels* true. Then, write all the evidence against it.

  Think about past wins, your strengths, and the times you've surprised yourself.

- **Destroy It:**
  Tear out the page, rip it to shreds, burn it, or stomp a mudhole in it. Whatever feels right. This is your way of saying, "This belief doesn't own me anymore."

Feel that spark? That's what happens when you take action.

You've just proven that even the thoughts holding you back can't stand up to the truth.

---

## DO THIS FOR 30 DAYS

---

Now take the second belief on your list—The Gatekeeper. Starting tomorrow, you'll work on rewriting and reframing this belief over the next 30 days, using some extra steps.

So set a reminder in your phone.

- **Write It Down:**
  Write the belief in your journal.

- **Say It Out Loud:**
  Speak this belief out loud, and then call it out for what it is: "No. That's not true. It's a lie."

- **List the Evidence:**
  List the evidence for why the belief *feels* true.
  List the evidence against it.

- **Reframe It:**
  Write a bold, empowering version of this belief.

  Example: "I'm not good enough" becomes "I'm learning every day, and every step forward matters."

- **Reinforce It:**
  Write the reframe on a sticky note and put it where you'll see it often. Maybe even take a pic of the note and set it as your phone background or create a daily reminder. Anything to keep the reframe in front of you.

  Say the reframe out loud every morning, replacing the old belief with this new truth.

- **Destroy It After 30 Days:**
  When the 30 days are up, destroy the belief just like you did with the first one. Tear it out, crumple it up, and burn it if you'd like.

Set a reminder on your phone right now—your DAILY exercise will start at the end of these 30 days.

---

## DO THIS DAILY

---

Here comes The Boss Fight: the hardest belief you've been carrying. By the time you finish your 30-day challenge, you'll be ready to tackle this one with confidence.

And just to ensure victory, we're going to add a few more steps to bring out the big guns.

- **Write It Down:**
  Write the belief in your journal.

- **Say It Out Loud:**
  Speak the belief out loud.
  Hear it for what it is—a lie.
  Then respond firmly: "No. That's not true. It's a lie."

- **List the Evidence:**
  List the evidence for why the belief *feels* true.
  List the evidence against it.

- **Reframe It:**
  Create a bold, powerful reframe.
  Example: "I'll always fail" becomes "Every step I take moves me closer to success."

- **Reinforce It:**
  Write it on sticky notes and place them where you'll see them.
  Set it as your phone background or create a daily reminder.
  Say it out loud every morning, focusing on this new truth.

- **Take Weekly Action:**
  Once a week, take a bold step that reinforces this belief.
  Example: Volunteer for a new opportunity or make a decision you've been avoiding and act on it.

- **Morning Visualization:**
  Each morning, take time to close your eyes and imagine yourself living out this new belief. Picture the actions you're taking and how your life feels as you embody this truth.

- **Evening Reflection:**
  At the end of each day, write down one thing you did that aligns with this belief. Celebrate even the smallest wins.

- **Destroy It When You're Ready:**
  You'll know when the time comes. When this belief no longer controls you, let it go—rip it up, burn it, or leave it behind. You've already won.

Stick to the work and these three exercises will build you some serious momentum.

Think about it, you've already conquered the **DO THIS NOW** step—*you did it, right?* That small win should feel like a spark, lighting the way forward.

As you take on the 30-day challenge, you'll prove to yourself that real change isn't just possible—it's already happening.

And when you commit to the daily practice, you'll find the strength to keep leveling up—one thought, one belief, and one bold step at a time.

**"If you lived honestly your life would heal itself."**

*- Dr. David Viscott*

Dr. Viscott makes a powerful point: living from a place of lies keeps you from living the life you truly want. This quote gives me so much hope because it reminds us that clearing out our head trash and tossing it in the dump is an act of honesty that honors both the life you want and the person you want to be.

And I don't want you to ever forget that truth.

So, grab a piece of paper—rip one out of your journal if you need to. Then, find the biggest Sharpie you can and write this in giant letters:

**I REFUSE TO KEEP LYING TO MYSELF!**

Tape it to your bathroom mirror where you'll see it every day, and call a friend to tell them what you wrote.

*Yes, seriously. Tape it to your mirror. Call someone.*

If you're not willing to do that, how can you expect yourself to do the work needed to rescue your dreams?

## THE EDGES OF EXPECTATION & THE CLIFFS OF COMPARISON

We took a hammer to the lies you've been telling yourself. We tossed that internal head trash, the limiting beliefs that convinced you to play small, to stay safe, to hold back from becoming the person you're meant to be.

But this journey is about to get more precarious.

Because while those internal lies are loud, there's another voice that often speaks even louder—the voice of everyone else around you. It's the voice that imposes all the roles and rules you never chose but somehow found yourself living out every day.

Welcome to the Edges of Expectation.

These are the invisible boundaries that others set for you, telling you how to think, how to act, and who they expect you to be.

The problem with living on these edges is that they can feel safe at first, like you're just following the rules, believing that you've mastered life in a way that meets everyone's approval.

But get too close to those edges, and you risk losing sight of your true self. You risk slipping into something equally dangerous—the Cliffs of Comparison.

At some point in our lives, all of us have walked those cliffs. The ones where you measure your worth against someone else's life, their success, their highlight reel.

You know, where you start doubting your own journey because it doesn't look like theirs. Where every step you take feels like it's being judged against someone else's so-called "perfect" performance.

Those cliffs are incredibly dangerous.

One wrong step, one moment of self-doubt, and suddenly you're in a free fall—spiraling into insecurity, doubt, and disconnection from yourself, all because you were too busy living someone else's life.

Most of us spend our lives balancing on these precarious edges, afraid to step off the path that someone else told us to walk. And afraid to not fit in. To be the one who disappoints, who chooses differently, who risks standing alone.

But the longer you live your life on these edges, the further you fall from who you really are.

Because others' expectations often shape our choices without us even noticing.

It's time to break free from those roles you never chose in the first place. To look at the life that's been shaped by others' opinions and dare yourself to take that first step back onto solid ground—ground that you choose.

Now, this isn't some reckless leap into rebellion. No, this is about recognizing when the life you're living isn't your own, when the choices you're making are designed to please everyone but yourself.

It's about seeing those expectations and societal pressures for what they really are—limitations that keep you small.

Boxes that suffocate you.

Scripts that aren't even yours.

But, before we can chart a new course, we need to understand how we ended up living out these roles that never felt like ours in the first place.

---

## WELL, HOW DID I GET HERE?

---

How many roles in your life have you consciously chosen? And how many of them were handed to you like a movie you never auditioned for?

Maybe it started with your family. You were the responsible one, the fixer, the one who always had to keep it together. Or maybe you were labeled the dreamer, the black sheep, the one who was never taken seriously.

You didn't choose those roles—they were handed to you, wrapped in someone else's expectations. Tied up with a pretty bow, as if there wasn't a turd in the box.

*Gross.*

And what about society?

It has this way of putting labels onto your life like they're tattooed on your forehead. Telling you what you should want, how you should act, and who you should be to fit in, to succeed, to be "enough".

Good student. Hard worker. Perfect partner. Selfless friend.

Sound familiar?

And then there's the culture we grow up in—the traditions, the unspoken rules, the ways of being that are passed down like family heirlooms. You're expected to take them on without question, to wear them like a uniform, to prove that you belong.

But belonging isn't about fitting into someone else's mold.

It's about knowing who you are when you strip away all those layers and stand naked in front of the mirror.

**"All we ever wanted was to look good naked, hope that someone could take it."**

*- Robbie Williams*, Bodies

We all want to look good naked, not just in the literal sense, but by being fully seen as who we really are. We want to stand there in our truth—unapologetically ourselves.

But for so many of us, the roles we play and the lives we live don't reflect that. Instead, we're compliantly following directives for roles that were cast for us long before we knew we had a choice.

But the truth is, you do have a choice.

You always have.

A powerful step to reclaiming your life is to see those roles for what they really are—constructs built on someone else's idea of what your life should look like.

---

## "ROLE" CALL

---

Let's name them. The things you were told you "Should" be. The roles you never even auditioned for.

Grab your journal and open to a fresh page—at the top, write this question: **Whose life am I really living?**

Start by listing out all the roles you play in your daily life. The ones that feel more like obligations than choices. The ones that you've carried because someone else expected it of you.

Maybe some of these examples, are you?

- **The Good Child:**
  Always responsible, never stepping out of line, making sure you never disappoint your parents.

- **The Fixer:**
  The person who's always there to solve everyone's problems, even when it drains your energy and takes away from your own needs.

- **The Breadwinner:**
  Pursuing a career or lifestyle because it's what's expected of you, not because it's what you're passionate about.

- **The Caregiver:**
  Putting everyone else's needs before your own, sacrificing your dreams because you've been told that's what makes you worthy.

- **The Peacemaker:**
  Always smoothing things over, avoiding conflict at all costs, even if it means never expressing your true feelings.

- **The Achiever:**
  Chasing success, status, or recognition because it's what society values, not because it's what lights you up inside.

These roles are often rooted in someone else's desires, not your own.

Sometimes, they're the roles that people in your life once played themselves, expecting you to carry on their legacy. Other times, they're the dreams they never had the chance to live, the roles they always wanted but never reached—so now they expect you to fulfill them.

But these aren't your dreams to rescue.

This exercise isn't about looking for someone to blame. Instead, it's a chance to see which parts of your life are genuinely yours and which ones you've been living out of obligation, fear, or inherited expectations.

And you can't change what you don't acknowledge. Until you see these roles for what they are—expectations disguised as choices—you'll keep walking a path that was never meant to be yours.

Now, under those roles, write this declaration: **I refuse to keep living someone else's life.**

Say it out loud. *Bonus points if someone is around to hear you.*

---

## THE IMPACT OF THOSE VOICES

---

Now that you've identified the roles you never chose, let's talk about how these external influences have impacted your decisions—sometimes without you even realizing it.

We like to think our decisions are our own, don't we? That we're steering the ship, calling the shots. But more often than not, those choices are quietly influenced by the voices of the people around us—voices that echo societal standards, family traditions, or the relentless hum of cultural norms.

It's subtle at first.

And deceivingly comforting.

You decide on a career path not because it lights you up, but because it sounds stable, respectable, safe.

You stay in relationships that no longer serve you because everyone expects you to. Leaving feels embarrassing—what would it say about you for choosing that relationship in the first place?

You go along with the plan, the rhythm, the routine because rocking the boat might mean you get tossed overboard—and you're terrified that no one is coming to save you.

And that sucks, because these so-called "choices" don't always feel like choices at all.

They feel like obligations.

Boxes that generations before you ticked off, telling them what's "right," what's "safe," what's "expected."

But what if, instead of feeling like a passenger on someone else's journey, you grabbed the map and charted your own path? What if you dared to step off the well-worn trails and forge your own way, even when it means venturing into unknown territory far beyond what others have mapped out for you?

This is your opportunity to take back control and reclaim your right to make choices that are truly yours—choices that come from your own values, your desires, and your vision for what your life could be.

The moment you start leading your own life, instead of letting others lead it for you, is the moment you begin to realize just how powerful you really are.

But when you're constantly measuring yourself against the world's standards, those Edges of Expectations and the Cliffs of Comparison, you lose sight of your own. And when you lose sight of that, you forget to ask yourself the most important question:

## What do I want?

When you can truly and honestly answer that, you need to protect it. And that's why we need some guardrails. Some boundaries.

---

## BOUNDARIES: THE ARMOR AGAINST EXPECTATION

---

In Part 2 of this book, we'll do a deeper dive into how boundaries can protect the dream you're rescuing. But for now, think of boundaries as the guardrails that keep you from falling off those dangerous edges. They're the lines that protect the authentic version of you that you're building.

When someone pushes their expectations onto you, or you find yourself comparing your life to others, ask yourself:

- **Does this serve my true self, or does it pull me back into living for them—or for their approval?**

- **Is this a boundary I need to reinforce to protect my goals, my dreams, my sanity?**

Give yourself permission to create distance from people, situations, or comparisons that don't align with who you know you are. Let your boundaries be strong and clear, and let them guide you away from the roles you never chose and toward the ones you do.

And when the world gets too loud, remember one thing:

## Tell it to shut the hell up.

We live in a world where everyone's opinions are amplified. Social media, family gatherings, even casual conversations—they all come with this undercurrent of judgment and expectation. It's easy to get swept up in what everyone else thinks you should be doing.

When the voices of others get too loud and the slick filters get too provocative, take a step back.

Turn off the notifications, walk away from the conversations, unplug from the things that don't serve you. Silence the noise so you can hear the only voice that really matters—yours.

The world will always have its opinions. The Edges of Expectation and the Cliffs of Comparison will always be there, tempting you to measure your worth by someone else's standards.

But when you start listening to your own voice—when you trust your values and your choices—that's when you finally see who you really are.

---

## I WANT TO BREAK FREE

---

Let's create space for your authentic self to breathe so that you can make the shift from living for them, to living for you.

For now, we'll scratch the surface to give you space to (re)discover yourself. It's important to start finding your voice early, even in small ways. By starting small, you're laying the groundwork for deeper insights as you move through this guidebook. After these light reps, we'll dive deeper into some of these concepts in Part 2.

### 1.  Redefine Success on Your Terms

The first step is to redefine what success means to you—*not* to your parents, your friends, or that influencer you follow on social media.

Strip away all those external definitions and ask yourself:

**What does success look like when I take away the spotlight, the applause, the approval of others?**

Does success mean freedom in your day-to-day life? Building a career that aligns with your passion? Creating a community that supports and uplifts you?

The moment you define success on your own terms, you weaken the power that the Edges of Expectation and the Cliffs of Comparison have over you. You start measuring your progress against your own benchmarks, not someone else's highlight reel.

## 2. Embrace the Discomfort of Disappointment

Breaking free from expectations means you're going to disappoint people.

Family members might not get it. Friends might question your choices. Society might think you're crazy for stepping off the beaten path. And you might even have to face ending a relationship that can't understand or support you.

That's okay.

It really is.

Disappointment is a sign that you're prioritizing your own needs over other people's comfort.

Embracing that discomfort is the price of authenticity. It's the cost of living a life that belongs to you, instead of one that's been scripted by everyone else.

Next time you're afraid of letting someone down, ask yourself:

**Am I willing to betray myself to please them?**

If the answer is no, then disappointment isn't a failure—it's a win.

## 3. Practice Radical Self-Permission

One of the biggest hurdles to breaking free from external expectations is waiting for someone else to give you the green light.

You don't need anyone's permission to live your life.

So, give yourself radical self-permission to:

- **Say no** to the roles that don't align with your truth.

- **Say yes** to opportunities that may scare you but also excite you.

- **Walk away** from relationships, jobs, or commitments that hold you back.

Radical self-permission means reclaiming your power to choose, without guilt, without apology. It's trusting that the only validation you need is your own.

## 4. Let Go of the Need to Explain

You don't owe anyone an explanation for the life you choose to live.

When you start stepping away from the expectations of others, people will ask why. They'll want to know your reasons, your logic, your plans. But your journey doesn't have to make sense to anyone but you.

Instead of getting tangled up in justifications, practice saying this:

### This is what *I* want.

No long explanations. No overthinking. Just a simple statement that honors your truth. The more you let go of the need to explain, the more you reclaim your energy for the things that matter.

## 5. Surround Yourself with Trusted Voices

Start amplifying the voices that actually lift you up.

Meaning, crank it up to 11.

Find people who see you for who you are, not for who they expect you to be. Surround yourself with those who encourage your growth, who challenge you to be your best self without trying to mold you into their version of "perfect."

These are the people who will stand at the Edges of Expectation with you, holding your hand as you leap toward your own truth.

If you're struggling to find those voices, remember this:

**You're not alone in your journey to live authentically.**

Seek out communities, mentors, or friends who've walked a similar path. Their support can be the difference between slipping back into old roles or standing firm in your new ones.

Breaking free isn't a one-time act—it's a daily practice. It's consistently choosing yourself and your truth over the comfort of fitting in. And it's not easy. Some days, you'll be tempted to fall back into old patterns, to retreat to the safety of roles you know.

But every step you take away from the life others expect of you is a step toward the life that's waiting for you. The life where you define what matters. The life where your choices are your own. The life where you're no longer living at the mercy of someone else's idea of who you should be.

So, let go of the need to perform, to conform, to explain. And take that step away from the Edges of Expectation and the Cliffs of

Comparison, knowing that the ground you're walking toward is solid, true, and entirely your own.

## THE POWER OF INTERNAL AND EXTERNAL CHANGE

We've been stripping away the lies you've been feeding yourself and tearing through the layers of limiting beliefs that kept you small. We dug out all that head trash and replaced the self-doubt with a clearer, more honest view of who you really are at your core.

Then, we turned our focus outward to see how those untrue internal beliefs are fueled by external pressures—the expectations of society, family, and culture that sneak in and shape your identity without you even knowing it. We stepped away from the Edges of Expectation and the Cliffs of Comparison, calling out the roles you've been playing out of obligation or fear of judgment.

This is where internal and external change come together as a powerful force. Internal change anchors you—it's when you stop running from yourself and start facing the personal truths that have always been waiting for you. External change is where you take that truth and live it out loud, making choices that reflect your authentic self—even if it means stepping outside the lines others have drawn for you.

This is where the transformation kicks in—when you turn those internal shifts into bold, unapologetic actions that shout your values to the world.

Think of internal change as the directive and external change as the execution. One without the other? It's like knowing the recipe but never cooking the meal, or like setting out on a journey without a map and wondering why you keep walking in circles.

You need both.

You need the self-awareness that comes from looking within and the self-leadership that comes from acting on that awareness. That's how you stop just talking about change and start living it.

## SO NOW WHAT?

Before we close this chapter, let's elevate that promise you made to yourself earlier.

Do you still have that paper taped up in your bathroom?

I hope you do—the one where you wrote, **I REFUSE TO KEEP LYING TO MYSELF!**

Now it's time to take that promise even further. You've refused to lie to yourself, but now you also have to refuse to let the voices of others—and how you compare yourself to them—lie to you, too.

The family pressures, societal norms, cultural expectations, and that nagging voice that whispers, "What will they think?"

You've got to face all those voices, all those expectations, and ask yourself: **Who cares?**

That freedom lies beyond the Edges of Expectation and the Cliffs of Comparison.

So, under your original promise, add this:

### AND I REFUSE TO LET OTHERS LIE TO ME, ABOUT ME!

Make those sentences your mantra. Every morning, every night, let those words ground you in your truth. Let it be the promise you keep to yourself, every day, as you choose the life you truly want to live.

# CHAPTER 2

## THE BEST POLICY

Now that you've cleared the mental garbage out of your head and your mind is clean, firing on truth, it's time to take things further.

We've got to use that clarity to fuel an unfiltered assessment of what you're good at, not so good at, and what you may never be good at.

In other words, we're going to dig into your strengths, weaknesses, and limitations—the very things that raise your self-awareness and allow you to know more about yourself than anyone else ever will.

Because not knowing yourself, is a dangerous game to play with your life.

**"Adam, if I know more about you than you know about yourself, I can control you."**

A dear friend said that to me once, and it rocked my world.

It came from my mentor, Dr. Doug McKinley, a man who's been a guiding force in my life for almost 15 years—*and the mental mastermind who wrote the foreword for this book.*

I remember when he said it, I thought, *Okay? So what?*

*Nobody knows more about me than me, right?*

But it wasn't long before my arrogance turned into concern.

*Wait a minute… nobody knows more about me than me, right?*

And then it scared the hell out of me.

Maybe I didn't know as much about myself as I thought. Maybe I'd given my power away too many times. Maybe I'd been controlled all along.

It made me realize that I'd been walking through life letting other people have a deeper understanding of who I was, than I did. And in doing that, I was handing them the reins to my life without even realizing it.

I decided that day I would never let anyone know more about me than I know about myself.

That's what was happening for you back in Chapter 1, wasn't it? You were living in a reality where other people's lies, expectations, and stories were running the show. And they did it easily, because they *seemed* to know more about what you wanted and needed than you did.

But if you want to live your life on your terms you need to fully own it, from the inside out.

This is so vital to rescuing your dreams. The more you know about you, the less anyone else can control you.

So, we're going to do an honest assessment and look at the whole picture: your strengths, your weaknesses, and yes, even your limitations. And by the end of this chapter, you'll know more about yourself than you ever have before.

Because honesty really is the best policy—especially when it comes to protecting yourself, from yourself.

---

## NEITHER GOOD NOR BAD

---

Let's talk about what you feel.

*I know, feelings are gross right?*

Well, maybe they're not gross. Because your feelings aren't good or bad. They just *are*. They're amoral. But somewhere we got a story in our head that some feelings like anger are bad and other feelings like happiness are good.

But the truth is, anger can be used for good. If you see something unjust, that anger could fuel you toward advocacy or starting a cause to help others who are marginalized.

And happiness doesn't always feel great either. I know that's weird to read but sometimes it feels uncomfortable, especially if you're not used to having a lot of happiness. If everything starts falling into place some people get anxious, waiting for the carpet to be pulled out from under them. So instead of enjoying it, they self-sabotage to bring their happiness back down to a level they're more comfortable with.

So, it's not about them being good or bad. It's really about knowing which emotions are more challenging for us to navigate and work with.

But why am I even talking about your emotions?

Because your emotions are helping to guide you through this life. They're informing you of what excites you, what brings you hope, and even what brings you down.

And if you're not careful in how you talk about your emotions, whether internally to yourself, or out loud to others, you could be in danger of them fusing to your identity. And if that happens the answer to "Who Am I?" might just be "I am anger."

But you are *not* your emotions. Your emotions are just indicators— signals that tell you how you're experiencing things in the moment.

Not who you are.

---

## FUSION

---

Susan David, a Harvard Medical School psychologist and expert in emotional agility, talks about this in her work. She calls it "fusion"—the moment we let emotions like fear, anger, or sadness stick to our identity like super glue.

Instead of saying, "I'm feeling angry," we say, "I AM angry." Do that enough times and you start to believe that's who you are at your core. Meaning you begin to believe that you ARE anger itself.

Good luck rescuing your dreams with that identity.

See, it's important that we keep our emotions exactly as they're meant to be, not facts, just information. And when you can look at your emotions as informative—just feedback—you can start using them instead of letting them use you. That's what emotional agility is all about. It's about recognizing that emotions are just data of how you're experiencing the world around you, not a permanent reflection of who you are.

Emotions are fun passengers in the car with you, helping you navigate. Some are getting off at the next stop, and others you'll be picking up.

But you're the one driving.

I want you to take a moment to practice not letting your emotions fuse to your identity. This is a muscle you can start building now, and it's going to serve you for the rest of your life.

Remember, your emotions are just indicators—they're not who you are. And I'm going to give you a simple exercise that'll help you separate the two.

### The "I'm Feeling" Exercise

Whenever you notice a strong and challenging emotion creeping in, whether it's frustration, anxiety, sadness, or even joy, do this:

**1. Name the Emotion:**

Literally call it out. Say to yourself, "I'm *feeling* [emotion] right now."

This shifts the language from "I *am* [emotion]" to "I'm *feeling* [emotion]." It might seem small, but this change in wording creates a gap between you and the emotion.

**Example:** Instead of "I'm angry," you'll say, "I'm feeling angry right now." You're acknowledging that the anger is present, but it's not defining who you are.

**2. Label It as Information:**

After naming the emotion, remind yourself that it's just information—like a dashboard light in your car telling you something needs attention. It's not the whole car; it's just a part of the system. Say to yourself, "This is just data about what I'm experiencing right now."

**Example:** "I'm feeling anxious right now, and this anxiety is telling me that I might be worried about something in my control—or maybe something outside of it." This turns the emotion into a useful signal instead of something overwhelming.

### 3. Ask What It's Pointing To:

Now that you've labeled the emotion as information, ask yourself, "What is this emotion trying to tell me about my current experience?" Is it highlighting a fear, a need, or maybe a boundary that's being crossed?

**Example:** "I'm feeling sad right now. This sadness is telling me that I might be experiencing a loss or disappointment. What is that, and what can I do about it?"

This might feel awkward at first, but you're learning to break the habit of fusing your emotions with your identity. And the more you practice, the easier it'll get. Make this exercise part of your toolkit. Use it when emotions rise up and start clouding your vision.

You'll be surprised at how much clarity you gain when you put some distance between yourself and those emotions.

So, the next time you feel something strong—whether it's anxiety before a big decision or frustration when things don't go your way—remember this: You are *not* that emotion. You're experiencing it, but it doesn't define you.

Once you grasp that, you unlock the ability to step back and evaluate. And this is critical for what we're about to do next, because an honest assessment requires a level head. It requires you to pull back from the swirl of emotions that often cloud your judgment.

Emotions can be loud, but they're not the whole picture. They're just pieces of the puzzle.

## AN OPTIMISTIC MIND

Optimism plays a huge role in how you see yourself, especially when it comes to handling challenges.

If your thoughts are cluttered with negativity or doubt, you won't have room for the truth about your potential. That's where optimism comes in—it's the bouncer at the door of your mind.

And pessimism isn't allowed in.

Now optimism isn't about toxic positivity and pretending everything's fine. Because sometimes, things aren't fine, and you need to know that. So, optimism has realism on the VIP list.

You see, real optimism acknowledges the challenges, but it frames them in a way that helps you grow. And it allows you to take things as they come, without rushing to assign a good or bad label on it.

It reminds me of the classic story about a farmer:

> One day, the farmer's horse ran away, leaving him without a horse. When his neighbors heard the news, they looked at him with sympathy and said, *"That's so unfortunate!"*
>
> But the farmer calmly responded, *"Maybe."*
>
> The next day, the farmer's horse returned along with a wild horse it had befriended. Now having two horses the neighbors looked at him with excitement and said, *"How fortunate!"*
>
> And again, the farmer said, *"Maybe."*
>
> Now since the horse was wild, the farmer's son set out to tame it. And while riding it in the field he was violently bucked off and shattered his leg. The neighbors who witnessed the accident gathered around the farmer and said, *"How unfortunate!"*
>
> And once again, the farmer said, *"Maybe."*
>
> The next day while his son rested his leg at home, some soldiers came to the village, drafting men for the war. They took one look

at the farmer's son and his broken leg and knew they couldn't recruit him. So, they carried on their way to the next house.

Hearing that the farmer's son was passed over to fight in the war, the neighbors exclaimed to the farmer, *"How fortunate!"*

The farmer simply replied, *"Maybe."*

We can learn a lot from the story of the farmer. Because maybe your challenges and setback are unfortunate.

And maybe they're not.

The only way to know is to keep moving forward knowing more of the story has yet to be told.

And you can do that by remembering and acting on three key optimistic truths:

## 1. Challenges Are Temporary, Not Permanent

When something goes wrong in your life, it's easy to think, *This is it. This is the way it's always going to be.* But that's most likely not true. The situation you're facing is usually *temporary*. Optimism allows you to view setbacks as just that—setbacks.

They're part of the journey, not the end of it.

Think about a time when something went wrong in your life. Maybe you lost a job or had a major fight in a relationship. It felt like the world was crumbling around you, right?

But here you are, reading this and knowing that moment didn't last forever, and neither will the challenges you're facing now.

This temporary mindset helps keep you from spiraling into despair when things don't go as planned.

## 2. Challenges Are Situational, Not Pervasive

Another key trait of optimism is recognizing that challenges are situational, not pervasive. This means that when something bad happens, it's just affecting *one* part of your life—it's not ruining everything.

Let's say you mess up at work. Maybe you miss a deadline, and your boss isn't happy. It's easy to think, *I'm a failure* or *I'll never get this right*. But the reality is that you had a bad moment at work. That doesn't mean you're a bad person, or that your entire life is off the rails. It's one situation, and it can be fixed.

This mindset allows you to compartmentalize problems, so they don't take over your entire life.

## 3. Challenges Aren't Personal

Finally, and maybe most importantly, optimists understand that challenges aren't personal. This means that when life throws something tough your way, it's not happening *to* you—it's happening *for* you.

That shift in perspective can change everything.

This is just like the farmer story. His neutrality in the face of both good and bad events isn't because he doesn't care—it's because he understands that life doesn't unfold in simple good-or-bad terms. He sees setbacks and successes as things that just *are*, and he knows that how he responds to them is what really matters.

In other words, it's not personal. Life isn't out to get you. The universe isn't plotting your downfall.

Sometimes, stuff just happens. And when you stop taking setbacks personally, you can start looking at them objectively and asking, *What can I learn from this? How is this helping me grow?*

## REFRAME YOUR SETBACKS

Let's make this sticky. Think about a recent setback in your life—something that felt like it knocked you down. Now, take a deep breath, and walk through these three steps:

1. **Recognize it's temporary:**
   This won't last forever. What will the situation look like a month from now? A year from now? Three years from now?

2. **Recognize it's situational:**
   This is affecting one part of your life, not all of it. What areas of your life are still going well?

3. **Recognize it's not personal:**
   This isn't happening *to* you; it's happening *for* you. I know that sounds cliché but it's true. What can you learn from this setback? How can it help you grow?

Write these reflections down. When you see your thoughts in writing, it gives them structure and helps you gain perspective.

As we mentioned earlier, optimism isn't about ignoring challenges or setbacks. It's about understanding that they're temporary, situational, and not personal.

Now, let's shift gears and talk about something you may have buried a long time ago ...

Your strengths.

## WHAT'S STRONG WITH YOU?

I know, it's usually easier to focus on your flaws. We're great at pointing out where we fall short, but we're awful at recognizing what we do well.

If you're the exception to this, I'm giving you 500 bonus points. Hold onto that practice and don't let go. And make sure that healthy pride doesn't turn into arrogance.

But if you're not the exception, then you need to own your strengths just as well as your weaknesses. And when you do that, you see clearly what makes you incredibly effective—what makes you, *you*.

Grab your journal because we're going to start with what's strong with you.

Not what's wrong with you.

Let's flex.

## 1. What Do You Do Well?

Let's start with the obvious. *What do you do well?*

What's something you can confidently say you're good at? Maybe you're a natural communicator, a fast learner, or you've got a mind for details.

Write it down. Don't overthink it. Just let the answers flow.

## 2. What Do You Do Better Than Others?

This one might make you squirm but, push through.

*What do you do better than others?*

Are you the one who stays calm in a crisis? The one who spots solutions before anyone else? The one who doesn't hold a grudge?

Acknowledge it. And more importantly, own it.

## 3. What Unique Skills and Talents Do You Have?

Let's dig deeper. *What are your unique skills and talents?*

Think about the things that come naturally to you, the stuff that seems harder for others. Whether it's strategic thinking or connecting with people on a deep level, these talents are where you *thrive*.

Don't ignore them.

## 4. What Do Others See as Your Strengths?

Sometimes, we're the worst judges of our own strengths. So, *what do others see in you?*

What compliments do you often get? What do people come to you for—advice, solutions, ideas?

Ask a few trusted people for feedback if you're not sure. They might see strengths you've been downplaying.

## 5. What Are You Proud Of?

What makes you feel proud?

I'm not just talking about winning a trophy. I'm talking about the small stuff too. What accomplishments, big or small, make you proud?

It could be a project you nailed at work, the way you handled a tough situation, or the fact that you kept showing up when it wasn't easy.

These moments are very easy to dismiss because they don't always feel significant to the world, but they matter to you.

## 6. What Do You Like About Yourself?

Yeah, it's uncomfortable to think about sometimes, but this is important. Don't brush it off. *What do you like about yourself?*

Maybe it's your resilience, your sense of humor, or the way you keep pushing forward no matter what.

Don't skip over this. Learning to appreciate your own traits is a step toward self-awareness, and power.

## 7. What Do You Enjoy Doing?

Last one: *What do you enjoy doing?*

What are the things you naturally gravitate toward? Whether it's problem-solving, organizing, or just listening to others, these activities hold clues to where your true strengths lie.

Because if you enjoy doing it, you've gotten your reps in.

BTW, the answers to these questions shouldn't be singular. Because I doubt there's only one thing you do well. Odds are, there may be many things. Or at least a few. So, look over your answers and give yourself some flowers. And water them by making sure you're really being honest about the many ways you're strong.

And it's okay and natural to see the same strengths show up in multiple answers. Pay attention if it does. It's showing you a pattern of something you excel in. And you can use that fuel to reignite your dreams.

### A Word About Exploring Natural Talents vs. Skills

*Natural talents* are what come effortlessly to you. Maybe you can draw well, or you've got empathy in spades. These are gifts. And when things come easy to you, you may do them a lot.

And when you do them a lot, you get good—really good.

*Skills* are learned. They're things you've developed through hard work and practice. Even if you weren't "born" good at something, you can still build the skills to get there.

So, don't get down if you feel like you're lacking in an area. With effort, almost any skill can be developed. The trick is knowing which strengths to lean into, and which skills are worth your time to build.

Now that we've flexed your strengths, it's time to face the other side of the coin: your weaknesses.

## WEAK IN THE KNEES

Ever felt weak in the knees?

It's that unsteady moment when life throws something at you, and your confidence wobbles. Maybe it's fear. Maybe it's self-doubt. Maybe it's the voice in your head saying, "This is too much."

The truth is, feeling weak doesn't mean you're failing. It just means you may have to try a little harder, dig a bit deeper, and play the long game.

You'll always have weaknesses. That's life. But the goal isn't to erase them all—it's to know them. To understand them so well that they lose their power over you.

Because when you know your weaknesses, you stop pretending they don't exist. You stop running from them or trying to hide them from the world. And that's when you take back control.

Some weaknesses will always be there, and that's okay. Others might be worth improving, but only if they truly matter to the life you're building.

Let's break it down, step by step, just like we did with strengths.

We'll uncover the areas where you can improve, and where you might need to find ways to work around them.

## 1. What Could You Do Better?

Let's start simple. *What could you do better?*

Think about the areas in your life where you know you could step it up. Maybe it's organization, communication, or follow-through.

What have your experiences shown you that you need to improve on?

## 2. What Do You Avoid?

*What do you avoid?* This one's a huge clue to your weaknesses.

What are the tasks, conversations, or situations you keep dodging? Is it being physically active? Tough conversations? Maybe having the focus on you makes your palms sweat?

Facing what you avoid will show you exactly where you need to focus.

## 3. Where Are You Less Skilled Than Others?

Here's another hard truth: *Where are you less skilled than others?* Where do you struggle compared to those around you?

Maybe being creative isn't your thing, or maybe you suck at multitasking. Don't put yourself down—just see where you need to improve. And if it doesn't align with your bigger goals? That's okay.

Recognizing it helps you decide where to spend your energy.

## 4.  What Do Others See as a Weakness in You?

Sometimes, trusted voices can provide valuable insight. It's up to you to decide which voices you choose to invite into the process.

Seek feedback from people you trust—those who have your best interests at heart and can offer a clear, honest perspective. Sometimes, the people around us have a better view of our blind spots than we do.

What feedback have you gotten from a trusted partner, friend, family member, or boss? These observations might be uncomfortable, but they're worth considering when they come from a place of care.

## 5.  What Do You Need to Face Up To?

Now, for the big one: *What do you need to face up to?*

What are you pretending not to know about yourself? Maybe it's a habit or behavior you've been brushing under the rug, telling yourself, *It's not that big of a deal.*

But you know, deep down, it's holding you back.

Instead of seeing your weaknesses as walls, use them as a compass. Weaknesses can point out where not to focus your energy. If a weak spot doesn't align with your bigger goals, give yourself permission to let it go. Focus your energy on the areas that matter most—the ones that will truly move you forward.

Reflect on the weaknesses you've uncovered from the questions in this chapter. Then, decide which ones are holding you back and need improvement. Let go of the rest, and focus your energy on developing the areas that will help you move forward toward your goals.

# YOU'VE REACHED YOUR LIMIT

Unlike weaknesses, limits aren't always things you can fix with enough effort. Some limits can shift over time, but others? They're fixed. And you need to learn how to navigate within them, not bulldoze through them.

Understanding your limits is key to avoiding frustration and burnout.

Keep fighting against them, and you'll just drain your energy. But if you accept them and work strategically within those boundaries, you'll free yourself up to focus where you can make the biggest impact.

## Temporary Limits:
## What's Holding You Back Right Now?

Let's start with the easy stuff—your temporary limits. These are the things holding you back right now, but they can shift with time, effort, or a change in circumstances.

- **Money:** Maybe your bank account is giving you the side-eye, telling you "Not today!" when it comes to your dreams. That's a temporary limit. You can create a plan to save or get creative with income streams to chip away at this.

- **Experience:** If you're lacking experience in a certain area, this is another temporary limit. You can fix it by learning, practicing, or gaining that experience over time. Break it down into steps— what can you start doing today?

- **Network:** If you feel like you don't know the right people to help you level up, don't worry—it's temporary. Relationships take time to build, but start reaching out, connect with mentors, and grow your circle. Do it with consistency, and you'll be surprised how fast this limit can shrink.

These limits don't define you. They're just speed bumps. With effort, planning, and persistence, you can blow right past them.

Don't get discouraged by where you are right now—focus on what you can change and then change it.

## Permanent Limits: What Won't Change?

Some limits are permanent, no matter how much effort you put in. Recognizing them helps you focus your energy on what's possible, instead of wasting it on what isn't.

- **Physical limitations:** Maybe you've got a chronic condition or a physical challenge that sets some boundaries on what you can do. This is a permanent limit, but that doesn't mean you're stuck. It just means you've got to work within those boundaries and focus on what you *can* do.

- **Personality traits:** So, you're naturally introverted or super detail-oriented? Great. No amount of self-improvement is going to make you a social butterfly or a big-picture visionary overnight. But that's okay. Stop fighting it and see if you can use those traits to your advantage.

- **Life circumstances that won't change:** We all have responsibilities that are just a part of life, period. You may be a parent, caregiver, or supporting someone with needs. These roles are mostly permanent, and your time and energy are limited because of them. But accepting these realities helps you plan better and be realistic with your goals.

Here's the twist—some permanent limits can actually be a strength that sets you apart. They make you unique.

Stay open to how a permanent limit could become leverage for momentum in another direction.

## Recognizing the Limits You're Avoiding

Here's the thing—sometimes we ignore limits because they're uncomfortable. We like to tell ourselves, *"If I just push harder, I'll get through this."* But ignoring limits doesn't make them disappear; it just sets you up for frustration.

- **What limits are you pretending don't exist?**
  Maybe you're telling yourself that you'll magically find more time next week, or that a physical limitation isn't holding you back as much as it is.

  Be honest about what's truly in your way.

- **What would happen if you accepted this limit?**
  Imagine the freedom of not fighting against it anymore. Recognizing limits frees you to focus on growth where it matters most and on what's within your control.

## Getting Outside Perspective on Your Limits

Just like your strengths and weaknesses sometimes it helps to bring in trusted voices when it comes to identifying your limitations. They can see things you might miss or give you that uncomfortable nudge you've been avoiding.

- **Ask for input from people you trust:** A partner, mentor, or close friend might help you see limits you've been dodging. It's not that they know better than you, but they can offer a perspective you haven't considered.

- **Are you overlooking something?** Sometimes, others can spot a limit you've been downplaying or avoiding. Trusted voices can give you the clarity you need to shift your focus.

Remember, limits aren't inherently bad. They're just realities that shape how you approach your goals—they're part of the map.

Some you can break through, others will redirect you—but every one of them helps shape the path to your goals. Recognizing them lets you move with purpose toward what truly matters.

## TAKING OWNERSHIP OF YOUR CHOICES

With the clarity you've gained from these last two chapters, you're ready to make intentional choices—aligning with your strengths and working around what might trip you up.

And you don't have to excel at everything to succeed—no one does. The key is focusing on what moves the needle in your life.

The people who seem like they've got it all figured out? They've learned to lean hard into what they're great at and stopped stressing over the rest.

Perfection is a lie. Clarity is truth.

Now that you've identified your strengths, that's where your focus needs to be. That's what will move you forward fastest.

As for your weaknesses? Not every one needs fixing. If it doesn't matter for your goals, let it go. If it's holding you back, decide whether to improve it or find a way to work around it.

Creating momentum requires directing your energy in the right places.

## FOCUS YOUR ENERGY

Grab your journal again. You're going to use what you've learned about yourself to make intentional decisions about where to focus your energy.

1. **Double Down on Your Strengths:**

Look at your strengths and ask: *Where can I double down? How can I use what I'm naturally good at to get results I want faster?*

2. **Drop the Weaknesses That Don't Matter:**

Look at your weaknesses and ask, *Which ones don't matter?* If a weakness isn't directly getting in the way of your goals, stop wasting time on it.

If it *does* matter? Make a plan to improve it.

3. **Work Within Your Limits:**

Take a hard look at your limitations and ask, *How can I work around them?* Maybe time is a major constraint—so how can you cut non-essentials from your day? If resources are tight, focus on smaller, realistic steps instead of trying to make a giant leap all at once.

Remember—this isn't a one-time deal. Life changes. What holds you back today might not tomorrow. And new strengths will emerge as you tap into your potential. Keep revisiting this process and keep adjusting your sails as you evolve.

---

## SO NOW WHAT?

---

Now it's time to uncover what drives you at your core.

Your values.

Because once you're clear on your values—you're in control. You'll know yourself better than anyone else. And that's when you'll finally be able to answer the question: *"Who are you?"*

# CHAPTER 3

## STAND AND DELIVER

Now, it's time to face the final piece of your identity puzzle.

In the first chapter, we uncovered the layers of lies, kicked the limiting beliefs to the curb, and you started to see yourself clearly for the first time in a while. This gave you a blank canvas—a fresh slate to paint a more truthful picture of who you are.

But it wasn't enough to just rip away those lies. We also had to dig into your strengths, weaknesses, and limits so you could see the whole picture. Why? Because clarity comes from seeing it all—the good, the bad, the stuff you'd rather not admit.

All of that work sets the foundation for what comes next.

Think of it like rehabbing an old, abandoned house. You can see its potential, but you can't start decorating or moving furniture in on top of mold, holes in the roof, and trash left behind.

Once it's clean, you see it for what it really is. You inspect it. You assess it. You figure out which walls can come down, what supports need to stay, what original wood can be restored, and what's outdated and needs replacing.

Then, you fill it with what matters—your colors, your furniture, the things that light you up. The rooms where you'll rest, the office where you'll grow, the kitchen where you gather, and the shelves for your favorite books and keepsakes.

And when you fill your life with what matters most—your values, your truth—you get to stand tall and not just say, "I'm home." But "I am."

## YOUR LIFE IS THE MOST VALUABLE THING YOU HAVE

Let's talk about this phrase: Stand and Deliver.

You've probably heard it before. In its original context, it was a phrase used by highway robbers in the 17th and 18th centuries as they held up stagecoaches. "Stand and deliver!" was a demand for valuables—give up your money or your life. It was a moment of high tension, forcing someone to reveal what they held as most precious.

But here, it's not about threats or demands.

Instead you're going to be standing tall and delivering the best, most authentic version of yourself to the world. The most valuable thing you have is your life—your truth, your core, and the values you live by.

And now it's time for you to deliver that. You're going to stand not just for yourself, but for the life you forgot you wanted.

Let's start by exploring how you see the world.

## SEPARATION VS. CONNECTION

There's something you need to understand: your worldview shapes how you live, how you see others, and how you see yourself. And there are only two ways to see the world: through Separation or through Connection.

## Separation Worldview

The Separation worldview is all about self-protection and self-promotion.

It's rooted in a scarcity mindset—the belief that there's not enough to go around, so you've got to fight for your piece of the pie. You've got to be better, faster, and stronger than the next person, because if you're not, someone else will take what's yours.

It's a "me vs. them" mentality, and it's exhausting.

People who live in a Separation worldview believe they're on their own. They think no one is coming to help them, so they have to do everything themselves. It's what my friend Dr. McKinley calls "rugged individualism," where the focus is entirely on self-reliance, believing that needing others is a weakness. They distance themselves from the truth that we're all in this together.

This belief leads them to live in constant defense mode. They're always watching their back, always calculating their next move, because deep down, they don't believe there's enough for everyone. They think life is a zero-sum game: for them to win, someone else has to lose.

But this rugged individualism isn't strength—it's Separation. It disconnects you from the very thing that gives life meaning.

## Connected Worldview

The Connected worldview is the opposite. It's the belief that we're all in this together and that there's enough to go around.

People who see the world this way understand that asking for help and offering it doesn't take away from their own success—in fact, it only multiplies it. They know that growth and achievement aren't individual pursuits but collective ones.

And it's important to understand that in a Connected worldview, collaboration and competition both have their place.

Competition can inspire growth and push us to strive for more, but its focus isn't on climbing over others to reach the podium. When viewed through a collaborative lens, competition emphasizes bringing out the best in everyone involved.

Now, this doesn't mean everyone will land on the podium or even cross the finish line—some may step away from striving altogether, and that's their choice. Supporting others means helping them rise to their potential, not doing the work for them or dragging them to the end of the race.

When approached with balance and intention, competition and collaboration together can create a space where trust, generosity, and a sense of safety thrive.

And if you find yourself lost in the wilderness, someone will come looking for you—because connection means you're never truly alone.

## Which One Are You?

So, which worldview do you believe you're operating from?

Do you find yourself constantly trying to protect what's yours, afraid that someone's going to take it away? Do you feel like you're always having to prove yourself? That's Separation talking, and it's draining. It keeps you isolated, always on guard.

Or do you believe that we're all connected, that there's enough for everyone, and that lifting someone else up doesn't mean you get left behind? That's Connection. It feels lighter, more secure.

It gives you a sense of peace, knowing you're part of something bigger than yourself.

Here's the thing: how you display your values will show you which worldview you're operating from. They'll reveal whether you're living in Separation or Connection. So, once we uncover your core values, we're going to circle back to this and see which worldview is guiding your life.

Now, why does this matter?

Because being aware of which worldview you've been operating from gives you the power to shift it if it's not working for you. And if you're operating from Separation, it hasn't been working for you.

Awareness allows you to live more holistically, giving and receiving while staying focused on the bigger picture, knowing your purpose is deeply connected to others.

But to make that shift, you need to understand what's really driving you. That's where your values come in.

## WHAT DO YOU VALUE?

We carry three types of values in our lives:

1. **Core Values**
2. **Chosen Values**
3. **"Should" Values**

These aren't all equal. Some guide us from deep within, while others are picked up along the way or pushed on us by outside forces.

We're going to focus on uncovering your Core values—the ones that are non-negotiable.

But before we dive into that, you need to understand the difference between these three types. Because once you get clear on this, you'll have the foundation you need to stand and deliver.

## Core Values – The Drivers

Your Core values are deeply embedded in who you are. No matter what happens, these values aren't going anywhere.

- **Your Life Scripts**

  These are the real scripts that guide you, not the lies we threw out in Chapter 1.

  They're the internal statements that fill in the blanks when you're asked something like, "Men are..." or "Life is...", or even "Money will ..." The answers to those questions come from your core beliefs, whether or not you're conscious of them.

  Your Core values influence everything.

  It's crucial to recognize these scripts because sometimes they can reflect mistaken beliefs or dysfunctional values. And if that's the case? Get help.

  Core values are tough to shift on your own, and it might take working with a professional to rewrite those scripts and replace dysfunctional values with healthier ones.

- **Inside-Out**

  These values aren't driven by your circumstances—they come from within.

  It doesn't matter if you're having the worst day of your life; your Core values still guide you. They shape how you respond to the world, not the other way around.

- **Nature and Nurture**

  Your Core values come from both who you inherently are and how you were raised.

  They're a combination of your unique wiring and the way things were modeled for you as you grew up. These values have shaped you over time, and they run deep.

- **Non-Negotiable**

  These are the values you'd be willing to die for.

  Yes, like fall-on-the-sword die for.

There's no compromise when it comes to your Core values. They're embedded in who you are, not something you casually switch out when things get tough.

And that's why sometimes, you just can't not speak up or take action when one of these values is challenged. They're that strong.

### Chosen Values – The Ones You Aim For

Chosen values are exactly what they sound like—you choose them.

They're the values you aspire to live by. You do your best to uphold them because they resonate with you, but—sometimes you slip. They're not as deeply embedded as your Core values, but they still play an important role in how you live your life.

- **A Balancing Act**

  Let's say you value both honesty and kindness. Now, imagine you're in a situation where you have to choose between being brutally honest and possibly hurting someone's feelings, or holding back the truth in order to be kind. Which one wins?

The value that causes you the most inner turmoil not to act on? That's most likely your Core value. The other that you'd be willing to compromise on, is most likely your chosen value.

- **We Do Our Best to Uphold Them**

Chosen values are the ones you select as important to you. You try to act on them as consistently as possible, but let's face it— sometimes it's tough to follow through.

- **Personal Resonance**

These values resonate with you and feel like they align with the person you want to be, but they're not always non-negotiable like Core values.

When push comes to shove, they might take a backseat to something more deeply ingrained.

- **Shame and Aspiration**

Here's the tricky part: we often shame ourselves for falling short of these values, thinking we're better at living by them than we really are. But in reality, they're aspirations, not deeply ingrained parts of who we are.

- **Selected for Fulfillment**

You choose these values because you believe they'll help you live a better, more fulfilled life. They matter, but they don't run as deep as your Core values—and that's okay.

When you find yourself torn between two values, unsure which one should guide you, that's when the difference between Chosen and Core values becomes clear.

You can't stand and sit at the same time. Ultimately, one of those will win.

## "Should" Values – The Ones Imposed on You

Societal "Should" values are driven from the outside in. They come from external expectations, not from within. They're superficial, surface-level, and shaped by what the world tells you is important. You think you *should* value ambition, success, or beauty because society says so.

But do they really matter to you? Or are they just what you've been conditioned to believe?

As we saw back in Chapter 1, these values often like to dress up as Core values, trying to convince you they're part of who you are.

But their costumes are as cheap as plastic, easily falling apart when examined closely. They might linger, loosely influencing your decisions, but they're not deeply embedded in your true self.

- **Superficial**

    These values stay at the surface. They don't shape who you are deep down—they only affect how you present yourself to the world.

    Like a mask you put on to fit in, they lack the authenticity and depth of Core values. They don't run your life from the inside; they just sit on top, keeping up appearances.

- **Driven by Society**

    These aren't values you've chosen for yourself—they've been imposed on you by societal expectations, trends, and pressures.

    They tell you what you *should* value, like ambition or beauty, even if those things don't align with your true self. You might feel pressured to adopt them because "everyone else is doing it," but they don't come from within.

- **Pressure to Conform**:

  There's a constant pressure to conform to these values. They tell you, "You should want this" or "You should act like that."

  Even though they don't define who you are at your core, they can still influence you from the outside, lingering in the background and making you question your choices.

Now that we've laid it all out, let's circle back to what really matters: your Core values. These are the values that form the bedrock of your identity.

Remember, they're non-negotiable. They're not chosen on a whim or picked up because someone else said you should. They come from within and guide everything you do—whether you realize it or not.

---

## UNCOVERING YOUR CORE VALUES

---

It's time to uncover what those Core values are, because until you know them, it's all improv.

There are four ways to begin uncovering your Core values, and when combined, they give you a clearer picture of the driving forces that allow you to live out what's most important to you.

Grab your journal …

### 1. Ask Trusted Voices

Start by getting some outside perspective.

Reach out to people who know you well—friends, family, colleagues, *lovers*. Ask them what they believe your values are.

And when you get their answers, don't judge them. Don't correct them. Just take it as information. A gift of insight into how others see you displaying what's most important to you.

Stay away from thinking that they're right or wrong. Just embrace getting a perspective from people who see you from the outside. Sometimes, we can't see our own values clearly because we're too close to them.

Let the feedback sink in and use it as a guide to reflect on your own sense of what matters.

## 2. Think Back to Your Childhood

Next, let's take it back to your childhood.

Between the ages of 6 and 12, you were probably more yourself than you are now. You didn't have as many filters, and you hadn't been told to be anything other than who you were.

Think back to that time—did you love finding bugs? Have a lemonade stand every weekend in the summer? Were you always drawing or reading?

Whatever it was, ask yourself: what value was I displaying when I did those things?

It may show you that you valued curiosity, entrepreneurship, creativity, learning, or something else.

Now ask yourself, of the values you just listed, which of them do you still do? Or would still do if your time and resources could support them? Think of it as what have you always done, that you will always do?

These traits often point to your core values—the ones that have stayed with you, even if they've been buried. They're still there, waiting to guide you.

## 3.  Reflect on Moments of Excellence

Now, let's look at the times when you've been at your absolute best.

Think back over the last three to five years—what were the moments when you felt like you were being and doing at your peak? Maybe it was when you led a project that went incredibly well. Maybe it was a personal situation where you were able to step up in a way you didn't even realize you could.

Now, list a few of these moments.

It doesn't matter if they're from your personal life or your professional life. The key here is identifying the times when you were on fire, when you were fully in the zone and acting in alignment with your true self.

Once you've got a list of those moments, ask yourself: What values were being displayed during those times?

Were you acting out of courage? Compassion? Integrity? This is where you start to see the patterns in your behavior and values.

These moments are like breadcrumbs, leading you to your core values.

Follow them.

## 4.  Make a List of What You Believe Your Values Are

By now, you should be starting to get a clearer picture of your values. You've gathered feedback from people who know you, reflected on your childhood traits, and identified your best moments. Now it's time to make a list of the values you believe define you.

Here's 15 to get you started:

- **Honesty**
- **Compassion**
- **Creativity**
- **Perseverance**
- **Loyalty**
- **Curiosity**
- **Integrity**
- **Courage**
- **Generosity**
- **Justice**
- **Respect**
- **Freedom**
- **Money**
- **Achievement**
- **Spirituality**

But don't stop here—there are way more values than what's listed, so spend some time honing in on the language that resonates most with you. Find the words that allow your values to come to light.

As of the writing of this book, you can search online for 'Brené Brown Dare to Lead list of values.' She offers a free resource from her book that's incredibly helpful.

However you chose to approach this, remember, this list is yours—no one else can define these values for you. They should reflect who you are at your core.

Don't overthink it—whatever comes to mind, get it down on paper. This is your raw material. You'll refine it soon enough, but for now, let it flow.

## 5. Narrow Down Your Values

First, gather all the values you've identified from steps 1 through 4—feedback from trusted voices, your childhood traits, moments of excellence, and the list you created.

Take a look at them all together and eliminate any redundancies or overlaps. If two values seem similar, choose the word or phrase that resonates with you most.

Now, it's time to get a little ruthless.

The goal is to narrow this list down to the values that truly matter—the ones you can't live without.

Start by narrowing it down to 10 values. Look at the list you've made and start eliminating the ones that don't feel as essential. Which ones are non-negotiable? Which ones are just "nice to have"?

Put a line through the "nice to have" ones, leaving the non-negotiables still on the table.

Once you've got your top 10, it's time to get even more focused.

Take it down to 5 values. And here's the thing—pay attention to how you feel when you're crossing certain values off the list. If it feels like no big deal to cross something out, that's a sign it wasn't core to who you are. But if you feel tension or stress when you think about crossing one off? That's a clue.

The values that are hardest to let go of are usually the ones that matter the most.

And if you're feeling bold, you can do what Brené Brown suggests and try narrowing it down to just 2 values. *500 bonus points if you do.* Those 2 will be the ones that guide everything else. They're the bedrock of your identity.

When you're done, go to a blank page in your journal. At the top, write: **These are important to me!**

Then, in big, bold letters, write your final values underneath.

These values are your foundation, and they deserve to be front and center. Look at them often—they will guide every decision, action, and purpose moving forward.

As you face new opportunities and choices ahead, ask yourself: Will this allow me to live out or display these values? If the answer is no, it might not be the right path.

Your values are your compass. Use them to navigate.

## REVISITING THE TWO WORLDVIEWS

Earlier, we scratched the surface of the two worldviews—Separation and Connection—and how they shape the way you see the world, others, and yourself.

Now that you've uncovered your Core values, it's time to take a closer look at how these values play into those worldviews.

But here's the thing—it's not just *what* you value that points to your worldview; it's *how* you choose to live through those values. The same value can steer you toward a Separation or Connection mindset depending on how you express it.

Take money, for example. Valuing money doesn't automatically mean you're stuck in a Separation worldview.

If your relationship with money is about hoarding it, constantly comparing yourself to others, and tying your worth to how much you've got, then yeah—that's Separation talking.

But if you see money as a tool to help others—fund startups, support education, or give yourself the freedom to travel and experience other cultures—then you're living from a Connected worldview.

Same thing with competition.

If you value competition because it proves you're better than everyone else and solidifies your position as a "winner" while others "lose," that's probably coming from a Separation mindset.

But if you value competition because it pushes you to grow, learn from others, and sharpen your skills, then you're expressing that value through Connection—using competition as a way to improve, not divide.

*See the difference?*

Let's dig deeper into how your values fit into these two worldviews.

## Separation Worldview and Your Values

Are your values driving you toward self-protection and always feeling like you need to guard what's yours?

Do you feel like there's never enough, so you're constantly competing to secure your piece of the pie? Whether it's money, success, love, or opportunity—do you feel like you're always scrambling to make sure you don't lose out?

That's Separation talking.

It sneaks into your life in all kinds of ways—guarded relationships, not trusting others, or keeping people at arm's length so you don't get hurt.

At work, it might look like seeing everyone around you as competition, a potential threat to your success.

In life, it's that "me vs. them" mentality—always calculating, always watching your back.

*Exhausting, isn't it?*

## Connected Worldview and Your Values

On the flip side, do your values reflect Connection? Do they express a belief that life is about lifting others up, that there's enough to go around for everyone?

When you're living from a Connected worldview, you're not worried about losing your slice of the pie, because you know there's plenty. Your values drive you, not the fear of missing out. You're secure in who you are, and you trust others to show up authentically.

In your career, you value collaboration over competition because you know someone else's success doesn't take anything away from you.

In life, you keep your hands open—you're not constantly worried about what others might take from you.

This worldview creates space—for abundance, for deeper connection, and for finding your purpose.

## Bringing It Together

So, it's not so much what you value, but how you choose to live out those values that shapes your worldview.

Are they pulling you toward Separation, where everything feels like you have to self-protect and self-promote?

Or are they driving you toward Connection, where growth and abundance are shared experiences?

Here's why this matters so much: later in the book, we're going to dive into discovering your purpose—and your purpose is deeply tied to others.

If you're operating from a Separation worldview, your purpose may feel shallow, cloudy, or even self-centered. It's hard to feel fulfilled when your world feels small and disconnected.

That's why it's so important to shift how you act on your values toward something more connected. When you operate from a place of Connection, your purpose becomes clearer, and your dreams feel more expansive.

When your dreams are only about you, they can feel small, like they're missing something. But when your dreams include others— lifting them up, sharing the journey—everything feels bigger, brighter, and more meaningful. That's the kind of life Connection offers.

---

## WHO ARE YOU?

---

Alright, we've dug deep into the values, the worldviews, and everything that came before. Now it's time to pull it all together.

In Chapter 1, we cleared out the lies, the stories, and the limiting beliefs that were clouding your view of yourself.

In Chapter 2, we took an honest look at your strengths, weaknesses, and limits, giving you a clear understanding of where you stand.

Now, with your Core values in hand, you have the final piece of the puzzle. These are the truths that guide you. No matter what happens around you, no one can take them away. You're not guessing anymore. You're not stuck in someone else's story or agenda. The lies are gone. The strengths are clear. And your values are rock solid.

Now, you can answer the question that matters most:

Who are you?

## This Is Not You

Here's the thing: who you are has nothing to do with your job, your relationship status, or the roles you play. Those things can change. You could lose your job tomorrow, your relationship status could shift, and your entire world could flip upside down.

But your *being*—the core of who you are—cannot be taken from you without your permission.

I had the privilege of attending a leadership summit on identity led by Jamie Winship, who has spent decades bringing peaceful solutions to some of the most conflict-ridden areas in the world.

Through his work, Jamie developed a powerful identity-based approach to transformation, helping people discover their true identity and unlock new levels of creativity and resilience.

At that summit, Jamie broke down an essential truth: you are not your job, your reputation, or even your ethnicity or religion. These are expressions of who you are, but they are not you at your core.

Here's what he clarified for us; **you are not:**

- **Your job** (what you do)
- **What people think of you** (your reputation)
- **What you have** (your possessions)
- **Your ethnicity** (your cultural background)
- **Your religion** (your beliefs)
- **Your sexuality** (your orientation)

You may celebrate and enjoy these things, there's absolutely nothing wrong with that, but they don't define your identity. A frog doesn't have to be told it's a frog. It just is, because its *being* informs its *doing*.

If you base your identity on having the role of a manager, what happens if you get fired? If it's centered around being a parent, what happens when your kids move out? If you focus your identity on being an athlete, what happens if you can no longer compete? Do you lose yourself in the process?

Absolutely. And many people experience the turmoil of this loss. Your hope in never losing yourself lies in the fact that these external titles, roles, or categories are not you. The answer to "Who Are You?" needs to reflect the unchangeable truths about you—your Core values and what's inside of you, not the temporary circumstances around you.

So, as you start this process, take a moment to reflect: What external titles, roles, or labels have you been using to define yourself?

Write them down.

And then above them write, **These are not my identity.**

## Illuminate

The answer to "Who Are You?" needs to hit home. It should feel like a declaration—something that speaks to your core and makes you feel solid, grounded, and empowered.

Think of it as a bold, unapologetic claim about who you are.

I get asked the question of "Who are *you*?" a lot when I do keynotes and group facilitations. At the end of my time, when I'm doing a Q&A, someone will usually raise their hand and say that this is such a hard question to answer.

And I agree. It's a very hard question to answer.

Then they'll ask:

*"So Adam, who are you?"*

And I get choked up every single time. Because my answer ignites something in my soul that feels like nothing else. Something begins to radiate from me when I speak, and I even begin to tremble a bit, fully in awe of what the truth of who I am feels like when it's spoken from my lips.

*"I'm sunlight."*

*"I illuminate the dark corners of people's lives so they can see what's keeping them anchored in place—so they know what's been holding them back from the life they forgot they wanted to live."*

*"I help you rescue your dreams so you can transform your reality."*

Notice how this example doesn't rely on any job title or external role. It's all about my core being.

I illuminate—that's what I do in any situation, regardless of my circumstances.

I'm a purveyor of hope—no one can take that from me.

And because my *being* informs my *doing*, the way I show up in the world becomes incredibly powerful. What I do isn't just an action—it's an expression of who I am at my core.

That's why I can confidently say: I'm very, very good at what I *do*.

And that's key here. The answer to "Who Are You?" is first about who you are, not what you do.

But when your being informs your doing, what you do carries incredible strength and impact. Your job could change, your relationships could shift, your circumstances could flip upside down—and you will still show up as 100% you.

And that's who the world needs.

## Stand and Deliver

Now it's your turn.

Grab your journal and write **Who Are You?** at the top of the page.

Then write, **I am ...**

Using the insights you've gained on your Core values and strengths, answer the question. Don't rush it—this is your foundation.

**Ask yourself:**

- **Does this resonate deeply with who I am?**
  When you read it, does it feel like coming home?

  Does it reflect the truths that have always been a part of you, even if they've been buried at times?

- **Does this reflect the person you're meant to be?**
  Does this statement align with the truths you're striving to embody with every choice, every action?

- **Does this inspire me to take action and live boldly?**
  Do these words ignite something in you?

  Do they push you to step forward with confidence and courage, even when things feel uncertain?

If your answer feels incomplete or off, don't force it. Give yourself permission to take your time. This isn't a statement you settle for— it's a bold declaration of who you are, something that resonates deep within.

Once you've spoken the words, write them on a piece of paper and tape it to your mirror—somewhere you'll see it every day.

Because this is who you are, and every day, you're stepping more fully into it.

---

## SO NOW WHAT?

---

You've claimed your identity. You've defined yourself from the inside out, without titles or roles getting in the way. Now it's time to live it.

Every time you look at that statement, let it fuel your choices. Let it guide how you show up. Carry it with you in every moment, in every decision, in every interaction.

Because your life—the way you live it—is the most valuable thing you can offer the world.

So step forward, fully grounded in who you are, and give the world your best.

Stand and deliver.

"When we are no longer able to change a situation,
we are challenged to change ourselves."

*- Viktor Frankl*

# PART 2
## WHERE ARE YOU GOING?

You did it. You faced the question that stops most people in their tracks: Who Are You?

And instead of hiding, you stood up and delivered a proclamation of your value, who you are—for the world, and more importantly, for yourself.

*You did do it, right?*

*Spent the time, dug deep, and cleared out all (or at least most of) the mental clutter holding you back?*

I'm proud of you.

And you should be proud of yourself too. There's nothing wrong with giving yourself flowers. Just be sure to water them.

Now that you've claimed your identity, it's time to take on the next big question: Where are you going?

Because being directionless is a poor plan for rescuing your dreams.

But before we dive into that, let's take a moment to reflect. What was the most challenging area of Part 1 for you?

Was it the raw honesty required to confront the lies you've been telling yourself? Or maybe it was the exercises, did they ask more from you than you were ready to give? Were you inconsistent? Did you skim through sections without doing the work? Did the process make you feel too uncomfortably exposed?

Maybe those challenges are telling you something.

Maybe they're hinting at what you may resist doing or what may be difficult for you in the chapters ahead. Change, *real* change—takes constant effort, and the truth is, rescuing your dreams and transforming your life is not for the faint of heart.

Remember what I said in the *"How to Use This Guidebook"* section: life isn't always convenient, and neither is this process. The exercises in this book should disrupt your flow.

They're meant to make you pause and take intentional action—right then and there. Not later. Not when it's convenient. *Now.* Because if you don't take action in the moment, you risk falling back into old patterns and missing the chance to create real momentum.

So, check in with yourself. If you felt resistance in Part 1, that's okay. But don't let that resistance hold you back from what comes next.

In Part 2, we're going to refine the vision you created in the *"You Are Here. You Want to Be There"* exercise. We're going to dig even deeper to get clear on where you're headed, because knowing who you are is only a third of the battle.

Now, you've got to map the path forward.

But, just like in Part 1, there are monsters lurking. If you're not careful, they'll derail you before you even get started. They show up in the form of unmet needs, a lack of boundaries, or a shortage of grit and resilience. They're sneaky, and they'll kill your dreams with their bare hands if you don't see them coming.

*Why do you think most dreams end up dead?*

But don't worry—you're not alone in your quest, others are on the way. Because, as with any journey of significance, it's best not to go it alone. People will be there to help you stay the course, give you the support you need, and hold you accountable when you feel like the road ahead is more than you can handle.

This part of the journey is creating a path that aligns with your values, your truth, and who you are. It's figuring out exactly where you're going and what you need to do to get there, all while staying on guard for the things that can knock you off course.

All that to say, Part 2 may be a heavy lift for some of you. And it's here where most people quit and start writing a story of why they weren't ready, it didn't work, it wasn't effective, or they just didn't have the time.

All of those stories are death blows to the life you really want.

But if you've already proven you can stand and deliver your best, then it's time to bring those dreams back to life and lead yourself to where you truly want to be.

# CHAPTER 4

## MAPPING THE PATH

So, now you know who you are. That's huge because most people go their whole lives never really knowing themselves.

But knowing who you are doesn't mean a thing if you're still wandering aimlessly through life.

**Where are you going?** That's the next question you need to answer. And not just with some vague idea, but with a clear, actionable vision—one that lines up with everything you've uncovered about yourself and brings your dream life into focus.

So, you're going to be creating a roadmap to get you from here, to there. Meaning, there's some work ahead that's going to require you to pace yourself and be very intentional about doing the upcoming exercises.

Get out your journal.

We're revisiting the **"You Are Here. You Want to Be There."** exercise. You started mapping out your dream life back at the beginning of this book, but now you've got more insight. So, it's time to make sure your vision is in line with who you really are.

# REFINING YOUR DREAM LIFE

When you first started, your vision back then might still have been clouded by doubt, fear, or other people's expectations. But now you know better. You've gotten clear about your values and what really matters to you.

So, the first thing we're going to do is review that dream life to make sure it's built on your truth—not on how you think you'll measure up to others or what you think they expect from you. And let's make sure it's not just a fantasy, or something that feels out of reach, but something that you can actually see yourself living.

Go back to what you wrote down—how has your clarity shifted since then? Is the life you imagined still what you want? Or does it need some fine tuning?

**Ask yourself:**

- What does my dream life look like now that I know more about who I am?

- Does this vision reflect my values, or am I still carrying someone else's expectations?

- Where are you in your dream life? What's your environment like? Does it continue to inspire you, or are you realizing that you're still settling?

- Who's with you? Who are the people around you? What kind of relationships are you building? Who's got your back? And who shouldn't be part of that picture anymore?

- What are you doing? What work or activities make you feel alive? What's lighting you up every day?

- How do you feel in your dream life? What's the emotional vibe of your future? Are you at peace, energized, fulfilled—or something else entirely?

Let yourself sink back into the dream for a bit. Walk away and reflect on it if you need to. Because the clearer you are, the easier it's going to be to create the roadmap that gets you there.

## DEFINING PERSONAL SUCCESS

Now that you've sharpened your vision, let's talk about defining what success looks like for you. Because if you don't define success for yourself, you're gonna end up chasing someone else's version of it.

And for many of you, that's exactly what you were doing before you opened this book.

The world is full of ideas about success. It tells you that success is a certain income, a prestigious job title, or even a certain type of romantic partner in your life. But none of that matters unless it's *your* version of success.

Your success should be measured by consistently living a life that's aligned with your values and purpose. Waking up every day knowing that you're living on your terms, not someone else's.

Living at *full* choice.

When you're not living at full choice it's like going into an ice cream shop and only seeing chocolate, vanilla, and strawberry as your options—when there's 31 flavors.

Full choice is knowing there are 31 flavors to choose from, to sample. And if you still choose vanilla, there's nothing wrong with that.

Here's a question you need to answer: When it comes to your dream life, what does success look and feel like to you?

I'm not talking about the surface-level stuff, like a fancy car or a big house (unless that genuinely lights you up). I'm talking about the more meaningful things—the things that make you feel deeply fulfilled, content, and alive.

So, let's take a minute and define what personal success means for you—not what just sounds good on paper, but what you truly want, free from the judgments of others, and even yourself.

**These should get you thinking:**

- **What does success feel like to you?**
  Is it peace of mind? A sense of accomplishment or contribution? Feeling connected to the people around you? Fulfillment in your work? Maybe it's all of them.

- **What kind of lifestyle reflects success for you?**
  Is it financial wealth? Is it more time to yourself? Enjoying meaningful work? Flexibility? Or maybe it's about structure, where everything has a place and purpose?

- **What are you doing when you feel successful?**
  Are you leading a team, creating something, teaching, traveling, or helping others? What are the activities that make you feel most alive?

- **Who are you with?**
  Who's around you in this successful life? Who or what type of people are supporting you, collaborating with you, or sharing your journey?

You've probably been carrying around someone else's definition of success for a long time. So, use this opportunity to wipe the slate clean and write down what really matters to you.

Because if you don't know what success looks like for *you*, how will you know when you've achieved it?

This is where so many people trip up. They end up chasing goals that don't actually make them feel successful. They hit milestones, check off boxes, and still feel empty because the goal wasn't aligned with their values, or their definition of success.

You need to know, deep down, what's going to make you feel like you're living your dream life. Otherwise, you're just running on a treadmill. You'll feel like you're moving but you never get anywhere.

So, get specific with this. The clearer you are on what success looks like for you, the easier it'll be to create the steps to get there.

But before we can map the path forward, we need to clear the roadblocks—the (not-so) hidden truths that are standing in your way.

---

## FACING (NOT-SO) HIDDEN TRUTHS

---

Now that we've refined your vision and defined what success looks like, we need to confront a tougher question—and a scary one: **What are you pretending not to know, that you know?**

And whatever the answer is that just popped into your mind, grab onto it. Don't let it get away or hide again.

I know it's uncomfortable. Because deep down, there's always something we know we need to face, but we keep burying it. Maybe it's a fear, an insecurity, or an unhealthy pattern that's too painful to admit.

But those hidden truths? They're blocking your path forward. And until you face them, you're not going anywhere.

Confront it.

Name it.

What's that thing you keep brushing under the rug?

It could be that you're stuck in a job you hate, but you're too afraid to leave. Or it's a relationship that's draining you, but you don't want to admit it because change is hard. Maybe it's the fact that you've been sabotaging your own success by avoiding the real work, thinking you can just skate by.

Whatever it is, we all have something. And if you don't face it, it's going to keep you stuck.

So, it's time to pick up your sword and slay the monster that you've been trying to hide. Grab your journal and write down your answer:

**What are you pretending not to know, that you know?**

Here are some swings you can start taking at it:

- **What fear or truth have you been avoiding?**
  Is there something you know you need to change but have been too scared to admit?

- **What limiting belief are you still holding onto?**
  Is there a lingering story you're still telling yourself that's keeping you stuck?

- **Where have you been playing small?**
  Are you not expanding your comfort zone because stretching it would require you to risk something?

Let me be clear: the things you're avoiding are the things that are holding you back the most. If you want to map a clearer path to your dream life, you've got to face the hard stuff head-on.

**If you're pretending that you don't hate your current situation, you're not going to be motivated to change it.**

Read that again.

**If you're pretending you don't need to work on your discipline or resilience, you're going to keep letting yourself off the hook when things get tough.**

Now, read *that* again.

The truth is uncomfortable. But it's also powerful. When you stop pretending, you take back control.

You can't fix what you won't face. And it's really hard to fight what you refuse to see.

---

## TURNING DREAMS INTO ACTIONABLE STEPS

---

Now, it's time to take all the insight you've been refining and turn it into something you can actually *do*.

Because in spite of what you've been told, knowledge is not power.

It's potential.

For it to become powerful, you need action.

This is where a lot of people will stop. They get inspired, they write down their dreams, they get that surge of motivation, but then it fizzles out because they never take the consistent steps to make it real.

And ultimately, they put the book down and never pick it up again.

Just like their dreams.

But here's where you're going to be different. We're not staying stuck in "someday" territory. You're going to break down that dream into *specific*, practical steps.

Think about it this way: your vision is the destination, and these steps are the road. If you don't have a clear path forward, you're just standing there, staring at the mountain, hoping you'll magically get to the top.

You won't.

And without a plan, you never will.

So how do we do this? We take that big, beautiful dream of yours and break it down into clear, actionable steps that you can work on right now—today, tomorrow, and the next day.

---

## MAPPING THE PATH FORWARD

---

Now it's time to turn your vision into a roadmap.

To make sure your steps are clear, realistic, and actionable, we're going to use backward planning—a process that starts with your end goal and works backward to define the steps needed to get there.

You'll also use the SMART goals framework to ensure your plan is practical and achievable.

Because as the old saying goes, *How do you eat an elephant?*

One bite at a time.

### Backward Planning: The End is the Beginning

Here's how you turn your dream into actionable steps:

## Start with Your Vision

Open your journal to your dream life. Imagine you've already achieved it—what does it look like? How do you feel? What's in place? This is your end **Goal**.

## Identify Key Milestones

What are the major **Milestones** that need to happen to achieve your goal? Break your vision into significant, manageable pieces.

For example:

- **Goal:** Switching careers.
- **Milestone:** Completing necessary training.

- **Goal:** Improving your health.
- **Milestone:** Reaching a specific fitness level.

- **Goal:** Deepening your personal growth.
- **Milestone:** Attending a transformative workshop, retreat, or coaching program.

## Break It Down

For each milestone, break it down into smaller steps—these are your **Actionable Tasks.**

- **Goal:** Switching careers.
- **Milestone:** Completing necessary training.
- **Actionable Tasks:**
  - Research career paths and industries that align with your skills and interests.
  - Identify certifications or training programs required for the new role.
  - Enroll in a training program and create a timeline for completion.

- **Goal:** Improving your health.
- **Milestone:** Reaching a specific fitness level.
- **Actionable Tasks:**
  - Schedule an initial consultation with a fitness trainer or coach.
  - Commit to daily exercise, starting with 20-minute sessions.
  - Track your workouts and progress weekly.

- **Goal:** Deepening personal growth.
- **Milestone:** Attending a transformative workshop.
- **Actionable Tasks:**
  - Research workshops or retreats that align with your goals.
  - Set a budget and plan travel logistics for your selected program.
  - Block time on your calendar for pre-workshop reflection.

### Applying SMART Goals to Each Step

Now that you've broken your vision into smaller, actionable steps, it's time to make sure each one is specific, measurable, achievable, relevant, and time-bound using the **SMART Goals** method:

**Specific**: Your goal should be clear and specific. No vague "I want to be healthier." Instead, "I want to run 5 miles in under 45 minutes."

**Measurable**: How will you track progress? For example, if you're aiming for a new career, how many networking meetings will you have each month? How will you know you've hit each milestone?

**Achievable**: Is your goal realistic given your current situation? For example, committing to an hour of study per day is achievable, but aiming to complete a course in two weeks might not be.

**Relevant**: Ensure your goals are aligned with your bigger vision and values. If improving relationships is a key part of your dream life, don't set irrelevant goals that distract from that.

**Time-bound**: Set a deadline for each step. Deadlines create a sense of urgency and accountability. Without them, it's too easy to push things off.

### Combining Backward Planning and SMART Goals

If your end vision is to improve your health, backward planning and SMART goals would look like this:

- **Goal:** Achieving optimal health and fitness.
- **Milestone:** Reaching a specific fitness level (e.g., running 5 miles in under 45 minutes).
- **Actionable Tasks:**
    - Schedule an initial consultation with a trainer.
    - Start jogging for 20 minutes a day, gradually increasing intensity.
    - Track progress weekly to measure improvement.
- **SMART Step:**
    - Jog 20 minutes, 5 days a week, for the next two weeks.

By combining backward planning and SMART goals, you ensure that every milestone and task is part of a clear roadmap and is practical, specific, and time-bound. This way, your big vision remains grounded in actionable, achievable steps that move you forward.

Now, let's dig a little more into this "time-bound" piece of your SMART goals.

Setting deadlines for your goals is about putting healthy pressure on yourself and using time as a tool to get it done.

Too many excuses are made around the idea of "wanting to feel like it" or "being in the mood" before taking steps. Those are excuses. Deadlines force you to increase your grit, stop spinning your wheels, and start making real progress.

And this is where Parkinson's Law comes into play.

## Parkinson's Law

Coined by historian Cyril Northcote Parkinson in 1955, this law says that work expands to fill the time you give it. So, if you allow yourself two weeks to complete something that could be done in two days, guess what?

You'll take two weeks to do it instead of two days.

Parkinson was actually poking fun at government bureaucracy when he said this, but the principle applies everywhere, from the workplace to your personal goals.

Challenge yourself: start using Parkinson's Law to your advantage by making the clock work in your favor. Shrink the time you give yourself to get stuff done.

Instead of saying, "I'll do it when I have more time" or "I'll get it done by the end of the month," ask yourself, *What if I had to finish it by the end of today?* Or, *What if I only had an hour?*

You'll be amazed at how fast you can move when the clock's ticking.

Not only will you get more done than you thought, but you'll also develop your ability to focus. Compressed deadlines push you to prioritize what really matters and cut out the distractions.

So, now that you've mapped out the steps with backward planning and set your SMART goals, use Parkinson's Law to compress the time you spend on each step.

Tighten your deadlines.

Embrace the discomfort.

Push yourself.

Here are some proven strategies you can use to work within tighter timeframes:

- **Timeboxing**: Give yourself a fixed amount of time for each task. If you only have 90 minutes, you'll get more done than if you give yourself the whole day. By creating these short windows, you force yourself to focus and work more efficiently.

- **Pomodoro Technique**: This involves working in focused bursts—typically 25 minutes—followed by a short 5 minute break. These sprints help you maintain high levels of concentration without burning out. It's amazing how much you can get done in a short, focused burst of energy.

- **Setting Deadlines for Small Tasks**: Even the little tasks— things like responding to emails or doing research—need deadlines. Give yourself 20 minutes to knock out a task, instead of letting it drag on indefinitely. Deadlines create urgency and keep you from wasting time.

These are next-level ways to leverage Parkinson's Law and maximize your time. You don't need two weeks for everything. Sometimes, two hours will do.

## Why Goal Setting and Planning Matter

Without clear goals and a plan in place, it's easy to drift.

You've seen it before—people with big dreams but no follow-through, always talking about what they're "going to do" but never actually doing it.

By breaking down your vision, using backward planning and setting SMART goals, you're creating a roadmap from where you are now to where you want to be. And I know it's not always easy, but it works.

Stick to it and you'll get there.

For some of you, this is the most work you've ever put in to designing and living the life you've always wanted.

But none of this matters if you don't follow through. Dreams don't come to life just because you wrote them down. It takes effort, consistency, and commitment every single day. The roadmap you've built? That's your guide. That's how you get from where you are to where you want to be.

And here's the best part: you don't have to figure it all out at once. Every step you take brings you closer, no matter how small it seems.

---

## CHECK-IN: ARE YOU READY FOR WHAT'S NEXT?

---

The work you've done here is big. You've broken down that huge dream of yours into actionable steps.

Now, it's time to ask yourself some important questions:

### Are you committed to following through?
This is where most people get stuck—they lose steam when it gets hard or inconvenient. Are you ready to do the work, even when it's tough?

### What's going to keep you accountable?
What will make sure you don't let yourself off the hook? It could be a friend, a mentor, or even just a weekly check-in with yourself. But accountability is key.

### What's the first step you'll take?
You've got the roadmap, but it only works if you start walking. What's the first action you're going to take today to move toward your dream life?

Write down your answers and then flip back to the first page of your journal.

Read what you wrote out loud.

**I'm committed to doing the work necessary for meaningful change in my life.**

Remember, this is going to take meaningful work. Challenges will come, there'll be roadblocks, and you may even get tired and discouraged.

But you've already proven that you've got what it takes. You stood up, faced your truth, and mapped out a plan that aligns with who you really are.

Now, take that plan and walk it out, day by day. The path might shift, and you might need to adjust as you go, but the point is—you have a path now. Keep moving, and you'll get there.

As the saying goes, *"I can't adjust the wind, but I can adjust my sails."*

---

## SO NOW WHAT?

---

I know this chapter shifted things to the nitty-gritty, and fleshed out the actual road forward. So, before moving ahead, let's recap the exercises from this chapter so you have everything in one place should you need to revise your map:

1.  **Refining Your Vision:**
    Revisit the "You Are Here. You Want to Be There." exercise and update your dream life based on your new clarity. Get specific about the details

2.  **Defining Your Success:**
    Write out what personal success looks and feels like for you— on your terms, not anyone else's.

3. **Confronting Hidden Truths:**
   Answer the question, "What are you pretending not to know?" Identify those uncomfortable truths that block your progress and face them head-on.

4. **Turning Your Dream into Actionable Steps:**
   Break your vision into 3-5 major areas, then list the key milestones and smaller steps for each. Set priorities.

5. **SMART Goals and Backward Planning:**
   Use SMART goals to ensure each step is specific, measurable, achievable, relevant, and time-bound. Then use backward planning to create a timeline that guides you from your dream life back to today.

In the coming chapters, we'll tackle some of the biggest obstacles that can knock you off course—unmet needs, lack of boundaries, and fear. But for now, start small and stay consistent.

No one rescues their dreams in a day.

# CHAPTER 5

## UNMET NEEDS ARE DERAILERS

You've been spending a lot of time thinking about what you *really* want—and that's great because it's the entire point of this book. Your dreams are your desires.

Success. Freedom. Living life on your terms. That's what you're after, and you should dream big.

But what happens when you chase after what you *want* and ignore what you *need*?

You crash.

Hard.

The problem is, you can't build the life you want if your needs are falling apart. I don't care how motivated you are or how clear your vision is—if you're not taking care of what you *need* to survive, thrive and grow, your dreams are going to stall out faster than a car running on fumes.

You can't work 12-hour days if you're operating on two hours of sleep. You can't build financial success if you're spending money faster than you're making it. And you can't have a healthy relationship if you're unwilling to make space for someone who values you.

Wants might get you out of bed. But if your needs are unmet, your wants will be too.

Your needs don't care about your timeline or your motivation. They just demand to be met. And if they're not being taken care of, no matter how badly you want something, they will take you off course.

And the truth is, for some of you, unmet needs have buried your dreams.

For others, meeting your needs *is* your dream.

But no matter which side you're on, *fulfilling* your needs is required to rescue your dreams.

## MASLOW'S GREAT PYRAMID

Alright, let me get a little academic on you. I'm not a psychologist (and I don't pretend to be one), but I've borrowed some wisdom from one—Abraham Maslow.

You've probably heard of him. He came up with a theory back in the 1940s that explains what drives us as human beings, and it's actually super relevant to the whole "wants vs. needs" conversation.

Maslow created a hierarchy of needs, which is basically a pyramid that lays out what people need in order to thrive.

The idea is simple: before you can focus on those higher goals—like becoming your best self and rescuing your dreams—you've got to make sure the foundation is rock solid. And that foundation? It's built on the most basic, fundamental needs.

Here's how Maslow breaks it down:

1. **Physiological Needs**: We're talking about survival here— food, water, shelter, sleep. You ignore these, you're dead. Everything else in life stops if your body isn't taken care of.

2. **Safety Needs**: After you've handled survival, you need to feel safe—financially, physically, and mentally. This is about security and stability. If your life feels like a constant crisis, you're not going to be able to focus on your dreams.

3. **Love and Belonging**: Once you're safe, you need connection. Relationships, community, support—those things that give you warm fuzzies and remind you that you're not in this alone.

4. **Esteem Needs**: This is where confidence and self-respect come into play, something everyone wants more of. You need to feel good about yourself and valued by others. Self-worth is key to pushing forward.

5. **Self-Actualization**: This is the pinnacle, the top of the pyramid where you're rescuing your dreams. It's the "living your best life" stage—but you can't skip to the top without building everything underneath.

So, why does this matter to you? Because if any of those lower levels are shaky, everything above them is going to crumble. You can't chase self-actualization if you're not sleeping, not eating, or feeling like your life is in chaos.

It's like trying to run a marathon on a broken leg—it's just not happening.

*Hold up, Adam ... if needs are so important, why didn't you bring this up sooner?*

Fair question.

It was crucial for you to first get clear on what you truly want. Building that dream vision for yourself—and feeling empowered to map it out—is the fuel that drives this whole journey.

But you can't build a reliable map if you don't see the obstacles in your path. If we're serious about bringing your dreams to life, then we need to get clear about what could slow you down, hold you up, or even kill your momentum.

And that's exactly why we're talking about unmet needs now—because if they're left unchecked, they turn into monster derailers.

So, we're going on an expedition to the top of Maslow's Great Pyramid, step by step, so you can see exactly where your needs are falling through the cracks and fix them. Because if you want to succeed, you've got to make sure you're not sabotaging yourself along the way.

For this, we're working with the classic 5-level model of Maslow's Hierarchy of Needs—physiological, safety, love and belonging, esteem, and self-actualization—even though Maslow later added more levels to the framework.

The 5-level model is simple, universal, and helps us focus on the core needs that most directly impact your journey.

Now this chapter might not hit every nerve for you, and that's a good thing. Not every need we talk about here will be unmet in your life. But before you skim past any section, take a beat. Ask yourself: *Could this area possibly be holding me back and I don't realize it?*

The exercises are here to help you uncover anything lurking under the surface. Because even if everything feels fine on the outside, small gaps in meeting your needs can quietly throw you off track.

Now, let's make sure your needs stay satiated.

# PHYSIOLOGICAL NEEDS: THE FOUNDATION OF EVERYTHING

First up, we're starting at the bottom of the pyramid: physiological needs.

It doesn't get more basic than this. You need to make sure you can function. If you're not eating, sleeping, and taking care of your body, you're already setting yourself up to fail.

No amount of positive thinking is going to make up for that.

If you're skipping meals, surviving on four hours of sleep, or living off coffee and energy drinks, you're not hustling—you're hurting yourself. You might think you're pushing through, but all you're doing is dragging a tired body toward burnout.

Some of you have even convinced yourself that you're lazy, unmotivated, or bored with life—when really, you've just been neglecting your own basic maintenance.

**Ask yourself:** Am I actually taking care of the basics?

- **Am I eating enough to fuel my body?**
  Are you consistently eating real meals that give you energy, or are you mostly surviving off quick fixes and junk food?

- **Am I sleeping enough to function?**
  If you're not getting the restorative rest your body and mind need, your productivity is going to suffer—and so will your health.

- **Am I staying hydrated and moving?**
  Enough water and exercise—two things people ignore when they're hyper focused on rescuing their dreams. But dehydration and lack of movement are silent killers of energy and focus.

If your physiological needs aren't met, nothing else works. Period.

If you feel this is an area you've been neglecting, then it's time to keep track of how well you're taking care of the basics.

**For the next week write down:**

- **What you're eating.**
- **How much sleep you're getting.**
- **How much water and movement you're getting.**

Once you've done that for a week, step back and look at the patterns. Where are you dropping the ball? Where do you need to adjust to make sure your foundation is solid?

Keep in mind that quality counts here. So whenever possible make consistent decisions to improve your nutrition, hydration, and even how much sleep you're carving out. Treat your body with the care it deserves.

Remember, every small shift you make is a win, and gets you a step closer to building a stronger, more resilient base for your dreams.

You can't skip this—it's literally the foundation of your entire pyramid, and everything else is built on this.

## SAFETY NEEDS:
## BUILDING SECURITY IN ALL AREAS OF YOUR LIFE

Now let's talk safety needs—because after meeting your basic physiological needs, the next step is creating security in all areas of your life: physical, emotional, financial, and even your time.

Safety needs provide the foundation that allows you to stop putting out fires and start building something that'll last.

Whether it's managing your finances, stabilizing your environment, or taking control of your schedule, safety needs are what give you the focus and peace of mind to move forward. Without them, you'll find yourself stuck in survival mode, constantly trying to keep your head above water instead of enjoying your swim.

Think of safety needs as the scaffolding that keeps the structure of your life stable. You can't build your dream life if you're overwhelmed by financial stress, time mismanagement, or the fear that the rug will be pulled out from under you.

Safety needs keep your life from falling apart. Without meeting them, everything crumbles—and there's no net.

## Physical and Emotional Safety

Safety needs start with feeling physically and emotionally secure. If you're constantly on edge—whether it's from a dangerous environment, unhealthy relationships, or overwhelming stress—it's impossible to focus on anything else.

**Physical safety** means having a stable, secure place to live and feeling protected from bodily harm.

**Emotional safety** means being in relationships where you feel valued, respected, and free to be yourself without fear of judgment, lies, or abuse.

**Ask yourself:** Am I physically and emotionally safe?

- **Do I feel physically safe in my environment?**
  Are there areas of my life—at home, work, or elsewhere—where I feel threatened or unsafe?

- **Do I have emotionally security in my relationships?**
  Are there people that you're walking on eggshells around or making you question your worth?

If these needs aren't met, everything else becomes harder.

Addressing physical and emotional safety is the foundation for creating the stability you need to thrive.

And I can't stress this enough: If you find that you're not safe physically or emotionally, don't delay in getting help.

**Seriously.**

**If you are not safe, your number one priority is to put this book down and contact a professional who can help get you the resources and support you need to secure this tier of the pyramid.**

Your life is worth reaching out to someone who can help.

## Financial Security

Let's get into money next, which is usually one of the biggest unmet needs people have.

When I shared my story of wanting to end my life at 23 years old, this safety need was so lacking, that it effected how I viewed my own self-worth. And it almost cost me everything.

Financial stress will mess with your head faster than anything else. You might be super motivated to rescue your dreams, but if you're constantly worried about paying the bills, keeping food on the table, and having a roof over your head, that stress is going to suffocate you.

You need financial security if you want to focus on building something bigger.

And no, I'm not saying you need to be rolling in cash to be successful. But you do need a level of stability that lets you achieve your goals without worrying if you're going to keep the lights on.

Financial safety is about having enough breathing room to make decisions based on growth, not survival.

**Ask yourself:** Am I in control of my finances?

- **Do you know where your money is going?**
  If you're not tracking your spending, it's time to start. You can't manage what you don't measure. If your money is flying out the door faster than it's coming in, you're setting yourself up for trouble.

- **Do you have a budget?**
  Budgeting is about making sure your money is being used in a way that supports your goals, not just disappearing into things that don't matter.

- **Are you living within your means?**
  I get it—sometimes we want to live like we've already made it. But if you're overspending and racking up debt to keep up appearances, you're building a future house of cards.

If you feel like this is an area of your life that needs attention, start with a **money audit:**

For the next month, track every single thing you spend money on. That means every coffee, every subscription, every impulse buy.

At the end of the month, sit down and ask yourself: Are your spending habits supporting your goals, or keeping you from reaching them? Where can you cut back? Where can you earn more? And where can you start investing?

The goal is to make sure your money is working for you, not against you. If your finances are a mess, you won't be able to focus on anything else, because that stress will always be in the back of your mind, eating up energy that could be spent on your dreams.

## Time Management

Look, full disclosure—time management isn't traditionally part of Maslow's safety needs.

But, it plays a critical role in creating stability.

And that's because like money, time is currency. And it's the currency we're given to spend on our actions, which makes it your most valuable asset. If you're not managing it well, it doesn't matter how bad you want it—you're going to run out of hours long before you rescue your dreams.

When you have clarity and control over how your time is spent, you create a foundation of stability that supports your goals and well-being.

Losing track of time or allowing it to be consumed by unimportant things can leave you feeling unsettled and disconnected from what matters most.

The problem is most people have no idea where their time is going. They think they're busy, but they're really just distracted.

And there's a lot out there vying for our attention.

All you have to do is check your screen time use on your iPhone to have a sobering wake-up call. Or count how many episodes of your favorite show you binged last week. Or even get honest about your "productive" procrastination—which gets things done, but not the things that really matter.

The key is knowing that you don't actually manage time—you manage yourself. Time moves forward no matter what. What you control is how you use it. Are you investing it in things that matter, or are you letting it slip through your fingers?

**Ask yourself:** Am I spending my time on what really matters?

- **How are you spending your time?**
  Are you prioritizing the things that get you closer to your goals, or are you stuck doing things that keep you busy but not productive?

- **Are you saying yes to too much?**
  You can't do everything. If you're spreading yourself too thin by saying yes to every opportunity, every request, or every shiny new idea, you're going to run out of this currency.

- **Do you have time for yourself?**
  Yeah, hustling is important, but so is recharging. If you're always running on empty, it's time to build some space into your schedule for rest.

**Time Audit:**

If a warning light is going off in your head for this need, then commit to tracking your time for the next three days.

And I'm talking every hour.

You might think you know where your time is going, but when you write it down, you'll see the reality—and it might surprise you.

Write down what you're doing during each block of time. Are you spending hours doom scrolling through social media? Getting sucked into other people's problems? Binge watching shows? Doing things that don't move the needle on your goals?

Once you've got three days of data, look at where you can exercise some self-control and reclaim your time for things that really matter. Then, build a routine that reflects your priorities.

Because if your time isn't supporting your goals, it's working against them.

## Stable Foundations

Let's bring it all together—physical safety, emotional security, money, and time.

These are the individual building blocks of safety, but stability is what happens when they all work together. It's the good smelling glue that keeps everything in place, giving you the space to think beyond survival and focus on growth.

Stability is all about creating a life where you feel grounded and secure enough to build something meaningful.

Check in with yourself regularly: Is your environment helping you grow, or is it holding you back? Are your routines giving you structure, or are they leaving you feeling scattered?

Stability creates mental, emotional, and physical space for your goals to thrive. Without it, your goals will start sinking—fast. With stability, you shift your energy from treading water to being able to swim across the ocean.

And here's the best part: when your safety needs come together to form stability, it's not just about you anymore. It frees you to start investing in the connections that matter—your relationships, your support system, and the people who lift you up and keep you going.

Because once you're no longer in crisis mode, you've got the bandwidth to focus on what truly drives your purpose.

So, now that we've laid the foundation of safety and stability, it's time to tackle the next level in the hierarchy: connection.

Listen, no one thrives alone, and love and belonging are essentials for growth.

# LOVE AND BELONGING: CONNECTION IS EVERYTHING

We're just going to scratch the surface here for now—enough to help you evaluate whether this is an unmet need in your life. In the next chapter, we'll dive deeper into how to not just meet this need, but turn it into a nurturing and sustaining part of your journey.

Because the truth is you can't do this alone.

I know that the myth of the "self-made" individual sounds empowering, but it's just that—a myth.

Nobody achieves real growth, fulfillment, or success on their own. Whether it's friends, family, mentors, or a supportive community, connection is what keeps you grounded, motivated, and moving forward when the journey gets tough.

But not all relationships are created equal.

Some build you up and strengthen your resolve, while others drain your energy or steer you off course. That's why the relationships you surround yourself with are just as important as the goals you're working toward.

Strong connections do more than provide companionship—they act as anchors when life's waters get rough and as sails when you need momentum. These are the people who remind you why you started, celebrate your wins, and hold you accountable when your steps falter.

But a wide circle of acquaintances won't serve you if the relationships lack depth or mutual respect. It's about quality, not quantity. True connection comes from a shared commitment to growth and authenticity.

### Identify Key Relationships:

Make a list of the people you interact with most regularly. These could be friends, family members, partners, colleagues, or anyone who has a significant impact on your life.

- **Do they encourage and support your goals?**

- **Do you feel energized or drained after spending time with them?**

- **Are they honest with you, even when the truth is hard to hear?**

Write down your observations. Who stands out as a source of strength and encouragement? Who might be holding you back? Recognizing these patterns will set the foundation for building a stronger support system.

Connection is essential—but creating relationships that truly sustain you requires intentional effort. It demands trust, vulnerability, and the courage to share your journey with others.

We'll talk more about this soon. For now, focus on identifying the people in your life who keep you grounded and inspired. This is your starting point—the first step toward building a circle that lifts you higher.

## ESTEEM NEEDS:
## BUILDING SELF-WORTH AND CONFIDENCE

We're almost to the top of the pyramid, so it's time to check out that little light of mine—well, actually, yours. Let's see how brightly it's shining as we go inward and move into Maslow's esteem needs—the foundation of self-worth, confidence, and respect.

This is where it gets personal because no one else can build your self-worth for you. It's on you—the way you show up, the promises you keep, and the actions you take. You need to believe you're valuable—that you deserve the success you're working toward—or you'll keep holding yourself down.

Confidence isn't something you're born with; it's something you build. Every time you follow through on a commitment, make choices aligned with your values, or face down fear, you're strengthening that foundation.

But confidence doesn't just grow from success. It's forged in failure. Because it's in failure that you learn that you're not as fragile as you feel.

Every time you stumble and get back up, you learn something new—about what doesn't work, about your resilience, and about your capacity to rise again. Those tough moments are where you truly grow. Where it's revealed what really matters to you. The things that are so important that nothing will keep you from it come hell or high water.

Think of confidence as a muscle. The more you use it through action and persistence, the stronger it gets. And here's another truth: confidence comes from self-respect. When you consistently show up for yourself and honor your commitments, you trust yourself more.

And that's where unshakable confidence is born.

If you're constantly breaking promises to yourself or letting negative self-talk run the show, it's like trying to drive with the brakes on. All you do is spin your wheels.

But with small, daily actions, you start to move ahead. Every time you push through doubt, stick to a routine, or prioritize your well-being, you reinforce your self-worth.

Progress doesn't require perfection—it just needs consistency.

**Self-Worth Audit:**

Let's audit how you're treating yourself. Take out your journal and answer these questions:

- **Where are you breaking promises to yourself?**
  Real talk—what have you been putting off or neglecting that you promised yourself you'd do?

- **How do you talk to yourself?**
  Is your inner voice kind and encouraging, or critical and harsh? Remember what you learned in Chapter 1, don't let head trash bury your worth.

- **What's one thing you genuinely like about yourself?**
  Come on, you know there's something—probably many things you like about yourself. You did a strengths exercise in Chapter 4 so if you need a reminder go back and look at how strong you are.

After answering, pick one area where you've been breaking promises and commit to fixing it. Start small. Whether it's showing up consistently, cutting negative self-talk, or forming a new habit, the goal is to rebuild trust with yourself.

## The Psychology of Self-Esteem

Let's take a step back and look at the science of self-esteem. For decades, psychologists have studied its impact, and the results are clear: high self-esteem is linked to success in nearly every area of life—relationships, career, mental health, and beyond.

Dr. Nathaniel Branden, often called the father of the self-esteem movement, found that people with high self-esteem are more likely to take risks, recover from setbacks, and pursue their goals with determination.

Why?

Because they believe in their value. They trust themselves to get the job done. And they're not waiting around for someone else to give them a sense of worth.

On the flip side, low self-esteem leads to hesitation, self-sabotage, and fear of failure. When you don't believe in your worth, every obstacle feels insurmountable, and you'll hold yourself back from opportunities because you don't think you're "good enough."

And when self-esteem is low, even small setbacks can feel like confirmation that you should give up.

And many do.

The work you do to build self-respect and confidence lays the groundwork for what's next, the top of the pyramid—self-actualization. This is where it all comes together, where you start living consistently in alignment with your full potential.

## SELF-ACTUALIZATION: LIVING AS YOUR AUTHENTIC SELF

Here we are—the top of the pyramid.

*What a view, huh?*

But here's the thing: if this capstone need goes unmet, it can derail everything. Self-actualization is what ties it all together—it's the bridge between the life you're living and the life you want. And without addressing the needs that form its foundation, you'll never reach its summit.

So, what does self-actualization really mean?

It's stepping into your authentic self—the person you've always been beneath the expectations, comparisons, and societal pressures. It's living in alignment with your values, doing what lights you up, and letting your life reflect who you truly are.

Self-actualization isn't about reaching a finish line or having it all figured out. It's a continuous journey—a process of becoming. Every decision you make, every action you take to align with your values, moves you closer to the life you want.

And the best part? Self-actualization doesn't require perfection. It simply asks you to show up as your authentic self, face challenges with confidence, and make choices that honor the person you're striving to be.

This is where you rescue your dreams and give them space to thrive—not someday, but now.

## SO NOW WHAT?

Before we wrap up, let's take a moment to reflect on the pyramid as a whole.

By the end of this chapter, you've gained the clarity to see why your life may have felt out of sync or unfulfilling and how unmet needs may have been holding you back.

Every level—physiological needs, safety, love and belonging, and esteem—works together to support self-actualization. If even one of these needs is unmet, it can derail your progress and leave you feeling stuck.

Think of this chapter as a compass. Whenever you feel off course—when fear creeps in, when doubt slows you down—come back here. Use this framework to reassess your needs and refocus your actions where they're needed most.

# CHAPTER 6

## THE POWER OF CONNECTION

There's a moment in every journey when you realize you can't do it alone.

Not because you're weak or incapable, but because connection is what makes the hard days bearable and the good ones worth celebrating. It's the people in your life who lift you when you stumble, remind you why you started, and push you to go further than you thought you could.

In my life, when I've faced challenges that felt overwhelming—monsters I hadn't yet conquered—just hearing someone close to me say, "You got this," has filled me with incredible courage.

In moments like that, those simple words mean everything.

But meaningful connection isn't automatic. It doesn't just happen because you know someone or because you happen to share the same space. Real connection—the kind that fuels your growth—requires trust.

And trust doesn't happen without vulnerability.

If the idea of being vulnerable makes you want to vomit, you're not alone. Most of us are taught to see vulnerability as a weakness, something to be avoided. But vulnerability is the heartbeat of connection. It's what allows people to truly see you and what makes relationships go from surface-level to life-changing.

Vulnerability is a bridge between connection and trust. And at first, it might feel shaky and unsteady, like you're going to be thrown off every time the path sways. But the more you cross that bridge, the more familiar it becomes. Your footing grows surer with every step, no matter the winds. Over time, what once felt uncertain becomes a steady path—with a strong sense of agility that can carry the weight of your dreams.

Without vulnerability, connection stays weak and unstable, unable to sustain the challenges of growth.

In the last chapter, we started exploring connection as a core need. You began identifying the relationships in your life—those that energize you and those that may hold you back.

Now, we'll go deeper into how meaningful connections— whether with family, friends, lovers, professional networks, or communities—can become your greatest strength.

You'll also learn how to turn vulnerability into a tool, not something to fear, so these relationships can truly sustain and uplift you.

Because at the end of the day, connection isn't just something we crave—it's something we need to thrive.

---

## AVOIDING ISOLATION

---

When we avoid vulnerability, we risk falling into isolation—and isolation is self-sabotage.

It doesn't protect us; it weakens us. Because isolation doesn't make you stronger—it makes you brittle. It cuts you off from the lifeline of support that fuels resilience, progress, and joy.

In Chapter 3, we explored the idea of the Separated worldview versus the Connected worldview. A Separated worldview keeps you locked in isolation, convincing you that every challenge must be faced on your own, because no one is coming to help you. It fosters the belief that asking for help is a weakness, and that struggling in silence somehow helps you grow.

But it doesn't.

Isolation is a thief. It steals perspective, leaving you alone with your doubts and insecurities, which grow louder the longer you sit with them.

Without someone to share the load, setbacks can feel insurmountable.

A simple roadblock starts to look like a dead end. You're left carrying the full weight of your goals, your struggles, and your fears, with no one to remind you how far you've already come.

The emotional toll of isolation is real, but it's not just about how you feel.

Studies show that isolation can have a hefty cost when it comes to reaching your goals. Research by the American Society of Training and Development found that individuals who share their goals with another person are 65% more likely to achieve them. That number jumps to 95% when they meet regularly with someone for accountability.

Why?

Because connection adds layers of encouragement, motivation, and shared commitment that simply don't exist when you try to do it all yourself.

And when someone else believes in you, it's easier to believe in yourself.

## WHAT CONNECTION BRINGS

Connection doesn't erase the hard days, but it can transform how you face them.

A strong support network gives you access to perspectives you can't find in isolation. And you need to have those voices in your life; people who challenge you, who hold you accountable, and who walk beside you through the ups and downs.

How many times have you doubted yourself, only to have a friend or mentor point out strengths in you that you couldn't see? Or even remind you of how far you've come when all you could focus on was how far you still had to go?

One of the most empowering things ever said to me when I was in a season of doubt was:

**"Adam, I see more in you than you see in yourself."**

Those words have forever stuck with me.

And now when I doubt myself, when I feel incapable, weak, and like I can't possibly make it through, I remember that there is still more in me—I just can't always see it.

Take a moment and think about this, who in your life reminds you of your strengths when all you can focus on are your weaknesses?

Who can you ugly cry in front of and not be counted as weak?

Who has seen you at your worst but consistently chooses to see you for your best?

Whoever comes to mind, and that beautifully safe and grateful feeling you get when thinking of them? That's the power of connection.

If someone came to mind, take a moment to put the book down, shoot them a text or give them a call, and let them know how much their support means to you.

*Really.*

*Do it now.*

Connection grows stronger when it's nurtured. So now is the best time to nurture it.

Isolation, on the other hand, feels easy because it asks nothing of you. No texts to send, no calls to make, no risks, no effort, no discomfort, and no personal growth. And it's also the surest way to stay stuck and keep your dreams buried.

Connection, on the other hand, takes courage. It requires a willingness to reach for others, when everything feels uncertain.

The choice to connect is one of the most powerful decisions you can make. Because when you build meaningful relationships, you gain more than just companionship. You gain perspective, shared strength, and a network of people who remind you that you're never walking this path alone.

Connection isn't just about receiving support either; it's about giving it, too. When you show up for others, you deepen the bonds that carry you both forward.

And as they say:

**"Shared happiness, is twice the happiness. Shared suffering, is half the suffering."**

# AVENUES OF CONNECTION

Breaking free from the solo mindset doesn't require a grand leap—just a small intentional step in the right direction.

Maybe it's taking an existing relationship a little deeper. Sharing a bit more of your fears, your hopes, or your struggles. Or you join a local group that aligns with your goals—a professional network, a book club, or a workout group. Sometimes, it's as simple as having an honest conversation with someone who knows you well but hasn't heard from you in a while.

If nothing feels like the right fit, create your own outlet. Invite people in your life to join you in a shared goal or regular check-ins. Build a circle of accountability that reflects your vision and values.

Connection doesn't mean sharing every detail of your life with everyone around you. It just means being intentional. Choosing the right people—those who energize you, encourage you, and challenge you to grow.

Not everyone will belong in your inner circle, and that's okay. The point is to start somewhere and to take steps toward connection instead of staying stuck in isolation.

So grab your journal and take note of anything that resonates as we uncover the support you need when it matters most.

## Family

Family relationships can be one of the most powerful sources of grounding, strength, and accountability. These are often the people who've witnessed your journey from the beginning. They know your quirks, your history, and most importantly, your potential.

One of your siblings might encourage you to take that leap you've been avoiding because they've seen you rise from setbacks before.

Or maybe a parent reminds you of the values you've always stood for, giving you clarity when the path forward feels foggy.

When family relationships are strong, they can be a fortress of encouragement when you're tackling a tough challenge or stretching your comfort zone to reach for an ambitious goal.

But, family isn't always simple.

Not every family relationship will lift you up. Some just suck.

That's why it's crucial to evaluate these dynamics honestly. Who in your family supports your growth? Who listens to you without judgment? Lean into those connections, even if it means prioritizing one relationship over another.

And for the family members who bring negativity or doubt, it's more than okay to set boundaries. Loving someone and protecting your energy are not mutually exclusive.

Strengthening these connections doesn't have to be complicated. It could look like scheduling a regular call or check-in, sharing your goals openly, or carving out time to simply be together.

These small, consistent actions can nurture relationships that leave you feeling supported, understood, and clear-headed.

### Friendships

Friendships are where life's joy and challenges collide. These are the people who celebrate your wins, hold space for your struggles, and remind you of your capability when you're tempted to throw in the towel.

A strong friendship has the power to anchor you in tough times and inspire you in the good ones.

Think about a friend who's always been in your corner. Maybe they've offered practical advice, like connecting you to resources, or simply sent a message on a bad day that reminded you that you're not alone.

These are the friendships worth pouring into—the ones that lift you up and help you grow.

To nurture these relationships, focus on mutual support. Be the friend who listens, encourages, and shows up. Maybe that means scheduling a weekly coffee catch-up, sharing something funny, or sending a simple text that says, "Hey, you crossed my mind today, and I'm rooting for you."

I can't tell you how much it means to me when a friend messages me just to say, "I was just thinking about you, how was your weekend?"

Friendships thrive on small, consistent gestures of care.

Lean into the relationships that leave you feeling energized and understood. And for the ones that feel draining or one-sided? It's okay to take a step back or exit them altogether.

True friendships should build you up and make your heart smile, not wear you down and give you anxiety.

### Community and Groups

Communities and groups connect you with people who share your goals, values, or interests. They're spaces where you can find belonging and encouragement—and often grow in ways you didn't expect.

I'm so grateful that I found a tremendous sense of community and some of my closest friendships when I started mountain biking.

I'd watch MTB videos from local YouTubers who not only showed me what trails I should explore, but also gave me the opportunity to connect with them and others when they would host group rides.

What I never expected is that those relationships I was making over a shared passion would extend beyond the boundaries of my local trails. Simply by engaging regularly in the comments section of videos, tagging people and trails in my Instagram posts, and following other passionate MTBers, I gained friendships around the world.

This deep connection was further fueled by me starting my own mountain biking channel where I would find regular support and encouragement from the MTB community.

And when it came time to host my first group ride, I was hoping that maybe a dozen people would show up. Instead, close to a hundred did.

That's the power of community and groups.

Take a second to think about it: What activities, goals, or values mean the most to you?

Where might you find people who share that passion?

Whatever comes to mind, start there—search online, ask a friend, or even start hosting your own get-togethers.

Through shared experiences, you meet people who don't just enjoy the same activities, they inspire you to keep showing up for yourself. Maybe it's a book club that sparks conversations challenging the way you see the world, or a professional association where you meet a mentor who shifts your perspective entirely.

Communities can also help keep you accountable.

For instance, joining a fitness group might be the reason you show up for that early-morning run. Or participating in a mastermind group could finally push you to tackle the goals you've been putting off.

There's power in shared purpose, and the energy of a group can remind you of your "why" when motivation feels distant.

And here's a tip from personal experience: to truly benefit from community connections, show up fully. Meaning, be present, introduce yourself, get involved, and invest in building relationships.

Who knows? That hiking group or book club you've been eyeing might just lead to the kind of connections that change everything.

### Professional Networks

Work can be much more than earning a paycheck. It can be a chance to connect with people who can inspire you to reach new heights. Professional networks offer accountability, mentorship, and opportunities for growth.

For instance, a mentor might guide you through a challenging career decision, offering advice from their own experiences. A colleague could introduce you to someone in your industry who opens doors you never imagined. Or a team member might encourage you to tackle a daunting project because they see the potential you haven't recognized in yourself.

For me, what started as someone in my professional network became a life-changing relationship.

Dr. Doug McKinley, started as a professional acquaintance of mine. I really admired his incredible mind and talent as a clinical psychologist and master certified coach.

One day we were having lunch together at an airport, waiting for our flight home. I remember picking his brain about self-image and identity. I was so captivated with his knowledge that I said, "I want to know everything you know!"

He paused. Looked at me for a moment, and then through his smile he said, "Okay Adam, if you're serious, I'll teach you everything I know."

That moment changed my entire life.

The wonderful people I work with 1-on-1, the organizations I'm engaged with, the leaders I help develop, the knowledge I have, and even this book, is all because of Doug.

Just one professional relationship became a life-long friendship, and the key that opened the door to my purpose.

That lunch at the airport taught me that a single conversation can change everything. You never know where a connection might lead until you take the first step.

Building professional connections can start with something as simple as attending networking events or participating in industry groups. Seek out relationships that encourage growth, whether it's finding a mentor like I did, collaborating with a peer, or connecting with someone who shares your ambitions.

These relationships are more than an opportunity to advance your career. They can be a supportive environment where you're encouraged to take risks, and uncover doors you haven't even thought to open yet.

## Romantic Relationships

Let's talk about lovers.

*Or lovaaaahs as some say.*

Romantic relationships, when healthy and supportive, can provide a deep level of trust and connection that enriches every other area of your life.

Partners are often the ones to see your best and worst moments, offering encouragement when you need it most and celebrating your victories as if they're their own.

For example, a partner might help you stay accountable to a personal goal by joining you in the journey—whether it's training for a race, creating a budget, or pursuing a creative project. They might also be the person who knows when you need a break and encourages you to rest without guilt.

But this is vital to remember, healthy romantic relationships don't exist in isolation—they thrive when both partners also maintain connections outside the relationship.

A partner can be an incredible source of support, but it's unrealistic for them to carry the full weight of your needs. No one has shoulders that big, and it's a tremendous amount of pressure that will inevitably lead to resentment and hurt feelings when they're unable to be all things to you.

**If you're in a romantic relationship:**
Reflect on how you and your partner currently support each other. Are there ways you could better encourage each other's growth or share your goals more openly?

**If you're not currently in a romantic relationship:**
Is finding a partner part of your vision for rescuing your dreams? If so, where might meaningful connections begin—through shared values, hobbies, or goals like the ones we've discussed in earlier sections? And if it's not a priority right now, that's okay too.

Remember, connection doesn't just come from romantic relationships. The support and encouragement you need can be found in family, friendships, professional networks, and communities.

No matter where you are in your journey, surrounding yourself with people who inspire and uplift you is vital to living your dream life.

# WHY IT'S HARD TO BE VULNERABLE

Each of these areas: family, friendships, communities, professional networks, and romantic relationships, offers a unique kind of support.

Some will ground you.

Others will push you.

All of them, when nurtured, can create a network that sustains and strengthens you.

And identifying these relationships is only the beginning. The key to unlocking their power lies in building deeper connections. And that means leaning into something we've touched on before but many of us still struggle with: vulnerability.

**"Vulnerability is the last thing I want you to see in me, but the first thing I look for in you."**

*- Brené Brown*

We all want relationships where we can be seen, heard, and valued for who we really are. But even though we all want it, no one wants to be the first to open up.

Brené Brown's quote captures this perfectly. We value vulnerability in others because it signals authenticity, trust, and courage. But when it comes to our own lives, we hesitate.

Why?

Because it's scary.

Vulnerability feels like standing naked in a spotlight with all our blemishes, saggy bits, and private areas exposed. It feels like handing someone the blueprint to our insecurities and hoping they won't use it against us.

The irony is that this very willingness to be open—to share our imperfect selves—is what fosters the kind of trust and connection we crave.

But someone has to go first.

If you've ever felt drawn to someone who shared a personal story or admitted a struggle, you've experienced the magnetic power of vulnerability. It's not their perfection that resonates with you; it's their honesty. It's the courage they showed in revealing what most of us try to hide.

And if vulnerability is the bridge between people, then ask yourself:

**Am I willing to step onto it first?**

I know it feels risky, and that's because it requires us to let go of control. When we open up, we can't predict how others will respond. What if they give us the stink-eye? Judge us? Or think less of who we are? These fears are hardwired into us. They're survival mechanisms left over from a time when belonging to a group literally meant staying alive.

Today, those fears hold us back more than they protect us.

They stop us from sharing the very parts of ourselves that could deepen our relationships. Instead, we build thick walls to hide our insecurities, only to wonder why we feel so alone.

But when you allow others to see your fears and struggles, you're not just showing them who you are; you're inviting them to do the same.

Vulnerability doesn't just connect us—it liberates us.

## How Do I Start?

Remember those names you wrote down in Chapter 5 when we talked through your Love and Belonging needs? The people who stand out as a source of strength and encouragement? That list is your starting point.

1. **Identify Who**

   Take a look at the groups and spaces we explored in **Avenues of Connection** and think about the relationships you could nurture in these areas:

   - **Family members** who've always been a grounding presence.
   - **Friends** who encourage and uplift you.
   - **Communities or groups** where you share common values or goals.
   - **Professional networks** that challenge you to grow.
   - **Romantic relationships** where trust and support can flourish.

But remember, not everyone has earned the right to hear your story. Deep and meaningful vulnerability requires trust. Look for people who have shown they're supportive, empathetic, and respectful of your boundaries.

Trustworthy people don't try to "fix" you when you open up—they listen, they see you, and they don't make it about them.

Once you've identified a few people who feel safe and trustworthy, take it a step further. Reflect on one thing you feel comfortable sharing with each of them—something small but honest.

This will help you prepare for practicing vulnerability in a way that feels manageable and intentional.

## 2. Start Small

You don't have to dive into the deep end. Vulnerability is like a muscle—it gets stronger with practice. Begin with something manageable. Share a minor setback or admit you don't have all the answers about a particular situation.

For example, instead of saying, "Everything's fine," try, "Honestly, I've been feeling a little off lately."

These small moments of openness build confidence and help you test the waters.

When you share a piece of yourself, pay attention to how the other person responds. Do they listen without judgment? Do they offer support?

Positive reactions reinforce your willingness to share more.

## 3. Take a Bigger Step

Once you've identified someone safe and tested small moments of openness, take a bigger step. Share something real and meaningful with them.

It doesn't have to be monumental—like sharing your biggest secret, but it does have to be honest.

For instance, you might say, "I've been feeling really self-conscious about the weight I've gained lately, and it's been hard to talk about," or, "I've been having a lot of anxiety at work and feeling like an imposter—like I'm in way over my head."

When you're open about your struggles or goals with someone you trust, you deepen the connection—and you invite them to help hold you accountable.

After you've shared, notice how you feel. Vulnerability often comes with a mix of relief and hesitation—sometimes even regret that you may have said too much.

It's what Brené Brown calls a "vulnerability hangover," and it's completely normal.

But over time, the relief will outweigh the fear, and the discomfort will transform into strength.

## 4. Reflect and Adjust

Not every vulnerable moment will go perfectly—and that's okay. Reflect on your experiences and adjust as needed.

If someone responds poorly, it doesn't mean vulnerability doesn't work—it just means you need to recalibrate who you trust. Use these moments as learning opportunities to refine your boundaries and grow.

**Ask yourself:**

- **How did it feel to open up?**
- **How did the other person respond?**
- **Did the interaction deepen your connection or reveal areas to improve**?

Remember, the goal isn't to be perfect—it's to practice. And vulnerability is a process worth nurturing.

### The Truth About Vulnerability

Vulnerability is transformative. It strips away the armor we wear to protect ourselves and replaces it with something far more powerful: connection.

By taking small, intentional steps, you're not just improving your relationships—you're reclaiming your power. Because when you choose to let others see the real you, you create space for deeper trust, shared strength, and the kind of relationships that will help you rescue your dreams.

And every time you practice vulnerability, you inspire someone else to do the same.

So go first.

Step onto the bridge.

And watch how vulnerability becomes not just a path to connection, but a foundation for accountability, shared strength, and the kind of relationships that will sustain you.

## CONNECTION AND ACCOUNTABILITY

Now, let's take your connections to the next level by exploring how building accountability into your relationships can supercharge the goals you set in Chapter 4.

You've mapped out your dream life and created SMART goals that are specific, measurable, actionable, realistic, and time-bound. But as we've uncovered, goals don't thrive in isolation—they need a support system to keep them alive.

That's where accountability comes in.

Accountability is an incredible lifeline when your motivation runs out. It's the friend who calls you out when you're slacking, the mentor who pushes you to aim higher, and the group that cheers you on while reminding you why you started.

Accountability transforms your goals from personal ideas into shared commitments that are harder to break.

Take those you've chosen to be vulnerable with and consider: Who among them could become accountability partners for your goals? Which of them can help you stay on track?

Accountability, when woven into your connections, becomes a force multiplier for your dreams.

## Examples of Accountability in Action

- **A Friend's Gentle Push**
  You might share your fitness goal with a friend who agrees to work out with you or check in weekly. Their encouragement will help keep you motivated on the tough days.

- **A Mentor's Perspective**
  If your goal is career-focused—like earning a promotion—find a mentor you trust to provide advice and challenge you. Being honest with them about your doubts or fears can deepen the relationship and make their accountability even more impactful.

- **A Group's Collective Energy**
  A writing group can hold you accountable for producing chapters, while also offering encouragement and a sense of belonging. Similarly, an entrepreneur group might provide valuable feedback and motivation to help you hit milestones for your product launch.

These relationships deepen your connections while fueling your progress.

## Strengthen Your Accountability Circle

Let's make this actionable. Here's how to connect your goals with accountability partners:

## 1. Start the Conversation

Reach out to these people with clarity and intention:

- "I've been working on something important to me and your perspective and support would mean a lot. Would you be open to helping me stay accountable?"

- "I really value your insight. Could we check in regularly to talk about my progress and get your advice?"

- "I've been thinking we could set a shared goal and help each other stay on track. Would you be interested?"

## 2. Build a Rhythm

Create a schedule for check-ins that works for both you and your accountability partner—weekly, bi-weekly, or monthly.

Set a regular time to meet, because no one's holding you accountable if you're both ghosting each other.

## 3. Celebrate the Wins

When you hit a milestone, don't just keep it to yourself. Share that success with your accountability partner or group.

Seriously, pop the champagne, fist-bump, or yell from the rooftops—whatever fits the moment. Progress is worth celebrating, and the people who've been with you deserve to share in that joy.

---

## SO NOW WHAT?

---

You're not meant to rescue your dreams alone.

No one is.

When you ask for help, for accountability, and for connection, you're not giving up. You're refusing to give up.

Now grab your journal and some tape.

On a fresh page and in big bold letters write this:

## I WILL NOT DO THIS ALONE!

Now tear it out and stick it somewhere visible: your bathroom mirror, your desk, your fridge—wherever it will remind you every day of this commitment.

- **Connection.**
- **Vulnerability.**
- **Accountability.**

These are the foundation of your dream rescue plan.

Each morning, look at the words you've written:

## I WILL NOT DO THIS ALONE!

Let these words remind you to always connect, to find strength in vulnerability, and to seek accountability for your goals. Let them ground you when doubt creeps in. And let them remind you that your dreams are worth rescuing.

And, that this isn't a solo mission.

# CHAPTER 7

## WEEDS AND WALLS

Imagine your life as a garden.

Each relationship, responsibility, and activity are a plant in that space.

Some are vibrant perennials, blooming joy and stability year after year. Others are seasonal annuals, meant to thrive for a short while before making room for something new. And then, there are the nasty weeds—those draining relationships, unnecessary commitments, and toxic habits that can overrun and choke everything else if left unchecked.

Boundaries are the tools you use to tend this garden.

They help you protect the precious plants that matter most, pull out the unwanted weeds, and create a thriving environment where your dreams can grow strong and resilient.

Now, this doesn't mean there won't be painful storms. Even with the best of boundaries at your disposal, cultivating your garden is what's really within your control.

The changing weather of life is not.

**"Pain is inevitable, suffering is optional."**

*- Haruki Murakami*

Haruki Murakami gives us some great fertilizer for our lives with this quote. And this applies not just to our personal struggles but to our relationships as well. Pain is a natural part of life—disappointments, misunderstandings, and tough decisions come with the journey.

The weeds of suffering, however, comes from ignoring what needs to change, allowing unhealthy dynamics to persist, or overextending yourself to meet others' expectations.

Boundaries are how you minimize unnecessary suffering.

They may not be able to control the painful storms, but they can protect your energy, time, and mental space so you can stay aligned with your purpose.

But setting boundaries can be challenging. It requires you to be clear about your priorities, hold others accountable for their actions, and, perhaps most importantly, hold yourself accountable for the choices you make.

So, let's tend to this garden.

Grab your tools, we're about to get our hands dirty exploring how to set boundaries in two key areas: with others and with yourself.

## PATTERNS OVER PROMISES

When it comes to setting boundaries, the first step is recognizing where they're needed. Often, this starts with evaluating the people in your life and the patterns that emerge in your relationships.

People like to promise us all kinds of things, because words are easy. And promises can be made with the best of intentions, but they mean little if they aren't backed by consistent action.

That's why a crucial principle in setting boundaries is this:

**Believe patterns, not promises.**

Ouch.

I know that's a sobering thought because for some of you, a key player in your life just came to mind—and not in a good way.

But hang in there, because if we're going to rescue your dreams, we need to rip the band-aid off.

Think about the people in your life—friends, family members, colleagues, even your partner. Do their actions consistently align with what they say? Or do they offer apologies and assurances only to fall back into the same behaviors that leave you drained, disappointed, or even heart-broken?

Patterns reveal the truth about someone's priorities, values, and ability to respect your boundaries. Promises, on the other hand, when not kept, can be a distraction and a huge let down. Because broken promises keep you hopeful, while the lip-service reveals inaction.

And that feels awful.

*But Adam, people can change.*

True. Everyone has the potential to change. And that's good news.

When promises are kept with consistency, a person's potential becomes their practice, and they form new patterns—ones built on reliability, trust, and mutual respect.

And relationships thrive when actions align with words.

But they die a slow and painful death when words are seeded but not watered. So always believe the patterns, not the untapped potential.

Those who genuinely value you will show it, not just say it. Over time, their consistent follow-through can transform your relationship into one that energizes rather than drains you.

Now, let's be clear—I'm not suggesting you write someone off at the first sign of imperfection. Relationships require effort, patience, and a lot of grace because no one gets it right all the time. Everyone stumbles, and part of maintaining strong connections is learning to navigate those moments with understanding and forgiveness.

But when an unhealthy pattern emerges and grows—when someone consistently disregards your needs, pulls you away from your goals, or causes harm, whether emotionally or otherwise—it's time to pause and reevaluate their role in your life.

A single weed might not seem like a big deal to you, but left unchecked, it can choke out the more meaningful plants you're trying to grow.

I'm not saying unhealthy patterns means cutting people off completely. Remember you're at full choice as to how you want to tackle this. But you should create strong boundaries that limit their influence on your energy, time, and mental space. That might look like saying no to plans that leave you feeling drained, setting clear expectations about what you're willing to tolerate, or simply choosing to engage with them less frequently.

In contrast, healthy relationships don't require you to constantly explain or defend your boundaries. These are the connections that leave you feeling supported and safe, where mutual respect is the foundation, and the relationship cultivates something healthy for everyone.

When someone consistently respects your boundaries, you don't have to fight to protect your energy—it's naturally preserved.

And it feels beautifully organic.

The goal of boundaries isn't to punish anyone; it's to create space for the relationships that truly nurture your growth and dreams. By identifying patterns, you're giving yourself permission to focus your energy where it matters most—with the people who show up for you in actions, not just words.

## RESPONSIBILITY AFFECTS ACCESSIBILITY

Sometimes, recognizing a pattern is only the beginning. The real challenge comes when you need to enforce your boundaries.

But, how do you hold the line without guilt or second-guessing yourself?

Author Lysa TerKeurst offers a valuable framework for this:

**Responsibility affects accessibility.**

This means the level of access someone has to you; your time, energy, and emotions should directly reflect how responsibly they handle their role in your relationship.

Let that sink in for a minute.

If someone hurts you, betrays you, belittles you, disrespects you, lies, or crosses your boundaries, you have every right to call them out on it. And when you do it's a chance for them to accept responsibility and change an unhealthy pattern in your relationship.

But, if someone consistently avoids accountability—ignoring how their actions affect you, refusing to respect your needs, or making excuses for harmful behavior—it's a clear signal that full access to you might not be warranted.

And here's the beauty of this principle: it encourages alignment in your relationships. By prioritizing mutual respect and responsibility, you create space for healthier connections while safeguarding yourself.

Lysa explains that healthy boundaries are like guardrails—they keep you from straying off course on the road of life. Without them, you risk veering into relational chaos, where resentment, frustration, and exhaustion take over.

But how do you adjust accessibility without guilt or feeling like a horrible person?

Start by acknowledging that protecting your well-being isn't selfish—it's essential.

When someone repeatedly demonstrates that they aren't willing to take responsibility for their behavior, reducing their access to you becomes an act of self-respect.

This might mean spending less time together, setting clear expectations about what behavior is acceptable, or, in cases where boundaries are consistently ignored, taking more definitive steps like blocking them on social media, your phone, or even limiting contact through shared personal networks.

I get it, sometimes setting strict boundaries can feel drastic, especially when you're not used to it. And depending on the length and depth of some relationships, this can feel like scorched earth, burning everything to the ground.

But that may be necessary not just to protect your dreams, but your overall safety and well-being too.

Keep this in mind, Lysa points out that boundaries aren't one-size-fits-all. The level of accessibility someone has isn't fixed; it can change as they grow and take responsibility. When someone begins to show consistent change—when their promises align with their actions—that's when accessibility can shift. So, it doesn't have to be set in stone, you can have flexible guidelines that evolve as trust is rebuilt.

Consider this: every time you say "yes" to someone who disregards your boundaries, you're saying "no" to something or someone that truly supports your journey. Because the boundary breaker is taking up a seat at the table that could go to someone more deserving of your energy.

### The Accessibility Audit

Take a moment to reflect on the key relationships in your life. Think about how responsibility and accessibility align.

In your journal, ask yourself:

- **Who consistently takes responsibility for their actions and respects my boundaries?**

   What relationships energize and support you? Who do you always love hearing from or spending time with?

- **Who shows a pattern of avoiding accountability or dismissing my needs?**

   Are there specific behaviors or interactions that leave you feeling drained?

- **How can I adjust accessibility to ensure my energy is protected and my goals stay on track?**

   Here are some practical examples that may help:

- **Limit Time Together:**
  Reduce the frequency or duration of interactions with people who consistently disregard your boundaries. For example, switch from weekly catchups to occasional check-ins.

- **Set Clear Expectations:**
  Clearly communicate what behaviors you will and won't accept. For example, "I'm not comfortable discussing this topic," or "Please don't call after 9 PM."

- **Decline Invitations:**
  Politely say no to events, commitments, or conversations that drain your energy. For instance, "I won't be able to make it this time, but I hope you have fun!"

- **Create Buffer Zones:**
  When engaging with difficult people, meet in neutral settings or group environments where the pressure is lessened, and boundaries are easier to maintain.

- **Reallocate Emotional Energy:**
  Focus more on relationships that uplift you. If someone constantly drains your energy, prioritize spending time with people who encourage and inspire you.

- **Digital Boundaries:**
  Adjust how and when you communicate online. This might include muting or unfollowing on social media, silencing notifications, or limiting phone calls and texts to specific times.

- **Physical Distance:**
  In cases of recurring boundary violations, consider creating physical space, such as reducing face-to-face meetings or choosing not to share living spaces.

- **Delegate Contact:**
  If necessary, involve a neutral third party for professional or

co-parenting situations, such as communicating through a mediator or shared app instead of direct interaction.

- **Set Time Limits:**
  When interactions are unavoidable, use time constraints to protect your energy. For example, "I can meet for 30 minutes, but then I have other commitments."

- **Seek Support:**
  Share your boundaries and concerns with a trusted friend, mentor, or counselor for additional accountability and encouragement.

The goal here is to create space for relationships that fuel you, not drain you. Because remember, when you set boundaries rooted in responsibility and accountability, you're not only protecting yourself but creating a pathway for healthier, more meaningful connections.

---

## THE WISE, THE FOOL, AND THE EVIL

---

So, we've looked at how patterns over promises reveal the truth of someone's actions and how responsibility affects accessibility.

Now, let's sharpen that lens even further.

If you want to set effective boundaries, it's crucial to understand who you're dealing with.

In his book *Necessary Endings*, Dr. Henry Cloud breaks it down perfectly. He identifies three types of people: the wise, the fool, and the evil. How they respond to truth determines the kind of role they play in your life—and we can use that insight to illuminate how your boundaries should be structured with them.

Not everyone in your life will respond to truth—or the enforcement of your boundaries—the same way. Some people embrace feedback and grow. Others dodge responsibility, make constant excuses, and shift the blame. And then there are those rare, harmful individuals who seem intent on destruction.

By understanding how to identify these types of people, you can get a clearer picture of who should have more—or less—access to you.

## The Wise

Wise people are the VIPs of your circle.

When you shine the light of truth into their life, they don't run or deflect—they lean in. They listen. They adjust their behavior to align with the truth. And they thank you for it.

Why?

Because wise people value growth over comfort.

They know they're not perfect (no one is), which means they're open to learning and getting better. And that makes them the kind of people who respect boundaries, too. When you set a boundary, they don't push back or dismiss it—they recognize its value and adapt.

I love being around wise people. They're the strongest and most courageous people you'll ever meet. They understand that in order to grow, you have to be open to hearing some uncomfortable truths and take life-changing action with that information.

### Examples of Wise People in Your Life:

- **Friendships:**
  You tell a friend they've been distracted during your hangouts—always checking their phone and making you feel like they're not fully present. Instead of getting defensive, they say, "Wow, I didn't realize that. Thanks for telling me—I'll work on being more present."

- **Family Members:**
  You gently explain to a parent or sibling that a certain comment hurt your feelings. They apologize, take accountability, and try not to repeat it.

- **Romantic Relationships:**
  Your partner listens when you say their teasing sometimes feels more hurtful and passive-aggressive than playful. They reflect on it, apologize, and adjust how they communicate.

- **Coworkers:**
  You give constructive feedback to a teammate about how they handle deadlines, and they respond with curiosity and action, asking how they can improve.

Wise people respect your boundaries and make it easy to maintain them because they're invested in keeping the relationship strong and healthy. Their actions show a consistent pattern of keeping promises and adjusting their behavior to honor the boundaries you've set. This builds trust and allows them to continue having meaningful access to your life.

Keep wise people close.

Cherish them and don't take them for granted. Wise people are rare, and they make you better. Invest in them. Learn from them. And most importantly, be one yourself.

## The Fool

Foolish people are some of the most draining to deal with.

When you shine the light of truth on a fool, they don't adjust their behavior—they adjust the light. They deflect, make excuses, or try to turn the conversation back on you.

Fools don't see feedback as an opportunity to grow. They see it as an attack.

Instead of reflecting on their actions, they double down on their behavior, creating a pattern of deflecting responsibility and dismissing your concerns.

**Examples of Fools in Your Life:**

- **Friendships:**
  You point out that they consistently cancel plans with you at the last minute, making you feel like they don't respect your time. Instead of apologizing and owning it, they say, "I don't see what the big deal is. I'm not stopping you from still going out!"

- **Family Members:**
  You try to set a boundary with a family member, and they dismiss your feelings by saying, "You're being dramatic," or "After everything I've done for you?"

- **Romantic Relationships:**
  You express feeling neglected and disconnected in your relationship. Instead of addressing your feelings, they accuse you of being "too needy."

- **Coworkers:**
  You highlight a mistake in a project, and instead of taking accountability, they throw someone else under the bus or say, "Well, if they would have been clearer, this wouldn't be an issue."

With fools, advice and feedback often fall on deaf ears. And that's because fools don't respond to wisdom—they respond to consequences.

That's why enforcing your boundaries is critical.

Personally, suffering the company of fools costs me far more than it's worth. Their patterns of deflection and avoidance drain my energy and rob me of time I could spend nurturing healthier, more meaningful relationships.

This is why I limit the access fools have to me—or remove them from my life altogether when necessary.

Remember, the patterns of a fool are unlikely to change unless they decide to grow. You can't do it for them, no matter how much you may want to. Set boundaries, enforce them, and give yourself permission to prioritize the relationships that honor your time, goals, and well-being.

## The Evil

Here's the good news: Evil people are rare.

Here's the bad news: If you have one in your life, they can wreak havoc.

Evil people don't just ignore the light of truth—they try to extinguish it. They aren't interested in accountability, growth, or connection. Their focus is control. They manipulate, deceive, and undermine, all while pretending to be on your side.

And sometimes they'll do it with a smile.

Evil people are intentional in their harm. Unlike the fool, who acts out of ignorance or selfishness, evil people actively work against you. Their actions aren't just careless—they're calculated. If left unchecked, their presence can cause lasting damage to your dreams, your peace, and your well-being.

### Examples of Evil People in Your Life:

- **Friendships**:
  A so-called friend shares your secrets to damage your reputation—or worse, spreads outright lies about you. When confronted, they gaslight you or deny any wrongdoing.

- **Family Members**:
  A toxic relative undermines your decisions, spreads rumors, or

tries to turn other family members against you. They thrive on creating division and drama.

- **Romantic Relationships**:
  A partner uses manipulation, gaslighting, or fear to maintain control in the relationship, dismissing your concerns and eroding your sense of self-worth.

- **Coworkers**:
  A colleague steals credit for your work, sabotages your projects, or spreads malicious gossip to damage your career while pretending to be helpful or supportive.

When dealing with evil people, there's no middle ground. You cannot reason with someone who thrives on harm. Trying to set boundaries with evil people often leads to them testing how much they can get away with.

Protect yourself at all costs. This might mean:

- **Cutting ties completely**:
  End contact, block them on social media, and refuse to engage.

- **Seeking professional or legal help**:
  If their behavior crosses into harassment or danger, don't hesitate to involve law enforcement or consult with a professional for support.

- **Creating a safe distance**:
  If cutting ties isn't possible—like with certain family members or colleagues—establish firm, non-negotiable boundaries and stick to them.

Evil people may offer counterfeit apologies when caught, but these aren't rooted in genuine remorse. They're a tactic to regain control and manipulate your trust. Don't expect true change. Expect them to continue deceiving, undermining, or retaliating in subtle ways.

Remember this: evil people want power and control, not connection. Your best defense is distance, clarity, and strength. Removing their access to your life is not an act of cruelty—it's an act of survival.

---

## PROTECTING YOURSELF FROM... YOURSELF

---

So, we've spent time focusing on the boundaries you need to set with others when it comes to rescuing your dreams, and that makes sense. While you can't control others, you can control how much access they have to your life and how they impact it.

But when it comes to boundaries, there's one person who's often overlooked. And they can be both the easiest and hardest to manage:

Yourself.

We're so good at excusing our own excuses, aren't we?

We're masters of rationalizing unproductive—and sometimes destructive—behaviors. And we're really good at talking ourselves out of doing the things we need to do and into doing the things we shouldn't.

How many times have you said to yourself:

*"I'll start fresh tomorrow."*

*"I'm too tired right now."*

*"I'm not motivated enough."*

*"What's the point?"*

*"Maybe later."*

We've all been there. Literally, every single one of us falls into this trap.

Our inner dialogue becomes a well-oiled excuse machine, turning procrastination into an art form and justifying the very behaviors that hold us back.

What's the end result of keeping that machine running? The self-defeating habits we want to break dig their roots deeper, while the dreams we want to rescue sit untouched.

And setting boundaries with yourself can often feel harder than setting them with others. Why? Because we treat ourselves as the exception to every rule. Unfortunately, we're also the ones who have to live with the fallout when those excuses pile up.

The truth is, those excuses—the lies we tell ourselves—have incredible power to keep us stuck in a life built on avoidance instead of intention.

But if you want the freedom to live the life you truly want, it's time to embrace the power of self-boundaries.

And it starts with how you frame your choices and commitments.

### The Power of "I Don't"

There was a fascinating experiment published in the *Journal of Consumer Research* that proves just how much words matter when setting boundaries with yourself.

In the study, researchers asked students to change their self-talk when faced with temptation. During the first part of the experiment, they were asked to imagine situations that tested their willpower.

One group was told to say, *"I **can't** do [X]."*

The other group was instructed to say, *"I **don't** do [X]."*

Then, the real test came. On their way out at the end of the session, every student was offered a treat: a chocolate candy bar or a granola bar.

The results were eye-opening.

The students who said, *""I **can't** do [X],"* chose the chocolate candy bar **61%** of the time.

The students who said, *"I **don't** do [X],"* chose the chocolate candy bar **36%** of the time.

*What?!*

Why did a simple shift in language make such a huge difference?

Simply put, because **"I can't"** feels restrictive. It's like a rule being forced on you—something you have to obey, but not something you necessarily chose.

But **"I don't"** is a personal choice. It's empowering. It's a declaration of who you are and what you stand for.

See, **"I can't"** feels like someone else is in control. **"I don't"** puts you back in the driver's seat.

Wild, huh?

The big takeaway from this is that the words you choose shape your identity. When you say, **"I don't,"** you're not just resisting temptation—you're reinforcing the kind of person you want to be.

*"I **don't** skip workouts,"* signals that fitness is important to you.

*"I **don't** allow distractions while writing my book,"* declares your commitment to focus.

*"**I don't** say yes every time someone asks me on a date,"* shows that you respect what's important to you in a partner.

Each time you use **"I don't,"** you're setting a boundary that aligns with your values and protects your dreams.

The students in the study proved that something as small as changing one word could shift behavior dramatically. If a single word has that much power, imagine what your life could look like if you started choosing language that empowers you.

### Ready? Set? Go!

I know self-boundaries can feel challenging at first, but they're incredibly liberating. Think of them as a superpower that helps you focus your efforts where it matters most and avoid the traps that slow you down.

If you want to make a massive impact in your life, here are some key areas you can start with:

- **Procrastination**:

  Establish a set start time for important tasks. Even if you don't feel ready, commit to starting anyway.

  *"I don't wait to feel motivated to do things that are important to me."*

- **Overcommitment**:

  Learn to say no when something doesn't align with your priorities.

  *"I don't say yes to people or things that pull me away from my goals."*

- **Distractions**:

  Designate specific hours for focused work.

  *"I don't check my phone while in a work time block."*

- **Rest and Recovery**:

  Set clear work hours and stick to them.

  *"I don't compromise my rest for the sake of hustling."*

The goal is to create boundaries that support your progress without making you feel trapped. Start with one area where you've struggled, experiment with setting boundaries, and adjust as needed.

### Hold Yourself Accountable

Even the best self-boundaries need follow-through to be effective. Accountability is what bridges the gap between setting boundaries and living by them.

Which means you have to commit to holding yourself accountable.

Now, hopefully you've enlisted other trusted voices to help with your accountability. But if you really want to rescue your dreams, you have to be the first person to consistently check-in with yourself.

Carve out time each week to reflect:

- **Are you sticking to your commitments?**
- **Are there areas where you're struggling or making excuses?**

Small, consistent course corrections keep you moving toward your goals.

And don't forget to celebrate your wins.

When you follow through on a self-boundary, give yourself credit. Maybe it's as simple as acknowledging the effort you've put in or taking a well-earned break. These moments are powerful for reinforcing your progress and keep your motivation alive.

If you slip up, it's okay. I know that no one sticks to their self-boundaries 100% of the time. There will be days when you fall into old habits or let distractions get the better of you. That's just the nature of life.

What matters is how you respond when it happens. Instead of spiraling into self-criticism, acknowledge the slip-up without judgment. Maybe you skipped your focus time because you felt overwhelmed, or you stayed up too late scrolling because you were tired and looking for comfort.

Recognizing the "why" helps you move forward without shame.

Once you've acknowledged what happened, take a moment and ask yourself: What led to the slip-up? Was there a trigger you didn't anticipate? Use this insight to refine your boundaries or adjust your approach.

The final step is to reset and recommit.

This is huge. Don't dwell on what went wrong; focus on what you can do next. Each time you reset, you're proving to yourself that your dreams and well-being are worth the effort.

And remember, believing patterns over promises applies to yourself as well. If you show a consistent—not perfect— pattern of forward momentum, then know that you're still making progress in spite of your own setbacks along the way.

# SO NOW WHAT?

You are at full choice to set your own boundaries.

Your boundaries are yours to define. They reflect what you value, how you protect your energy, and the kind of life you want to cultivate.

No one else has the right to decide those for you.

No one.

Not even your partner.

I know this can feel counterintuitive, but it's the truth. No one has the right to tell you what your boundaries should be for your life:

What you're allowed to watch.
What you're allowed to read.
What you're allowed to look at.
What you're allowed to eat.
What you're allowed to drink
How you're allowed to dress.
Who you're allowed to talk to.
How you're allowed to talk to them.
How much you're allowed to talk to them.
What you're allowed to say.
How you're allowed to say it.
What you're allowed to believe.
What you're allowed to think.
What you're allowed to feel.

And on.
And on.
And on.

And the same is true in reverse. Just as no one has the right to dictate your boundaries, you don't get to decide someone else's. People have their own reasons for the choices they make. You may not understand them, but they're not yours to control.

This becomes especially important in relationships.

If your boundaries make someone uncomfortable, it's essential to communicate openly. Let them decide if they can live within the space you've created for yourself. Similarly, if someone's boundaries don't align with your values or comfort level, you have every right to decide if that relationship still fits into your life.

Living at full choice means respecting both your boundaries and the boundaries of others. This mutual respect creates clarity and frees you to live authentically.

But we're all human. Which means there will be moments when it feels easier to let your boundaries slip. When the pull of old habits, distractions, or the comfort of people-pleasing threatens to pull you off track. In those moments, pause. Remind yourself why you set those boundaries in the first place.

Every boundary you honor is an act of care for your dreams.

Boundaries are the tools that help you tend the garden of your life. They allow you to nurture the perennials, welcome the annuals, and keep the weeds from taking over. With each boundary, you're creating a space where your dreams can take root and flourish.

So, grab your tools. Pull on your gloves. And keep cultivating the life you've always wanted.

# CHAPTER 8

## YOUR WINGS AREN'T MADE OF FEAR

I love birds.

*Which is why they're all over this book.*

Especially magpies, crows, and ravens.

There's something so fascinating about their intelligence. They craft tools to access hard-to-reach food, deceive humans with decoy nests to protect their young, and even recognize individual faces— remembering exactly who's treated them kindly and who hasn't.

Meaning they can remember who's been naughty and who's been nice to them.

And they hold grudges.

But these corvids aren't born knowing how to do these things. They learn them through trial and error—through successes and failures. Moving through their fears of not having enough food, keeping predators from finding their nest, or even learning who to trust. And through this process they grow wiser, stronger, expanding their comfort zones and thriving—not just on their own, but within the support of their flock.

Just like we do.

And just like us, one of the first things they have to learn, is what their wings are made of.

And more importantly, what they're for.

When a fledgling raven first leaves the nest, its initial attempts at flight are, well, messy. Wings flapping like mad, it stumbles through the air more than it soars, barely making it to a low branch—or, more likely, crashing to the ground.

But that's exactly how it's supposed to happen.

Those clumsy starts are necessary for learning. Each awkward landing builds agility. Each wobbly attempt teaches it something new about balance, wind, and how to stay aloft a little longer next time.

And all the while, the parents are nearby. They don't helicopter in to save the day every time their fledgling struggles, but you can feel their tension. They watch, squawking softly, perched close enough to step in if things get too dangerous. You can almost see the conflict in their posture: the nervous energy of wanting to help versus the wisdom of knowing they shouldn't. They understand that the struggle is necessary. And if they swoop in too soon, their young won't gain the confidence or strength needed to truly fly.

Then, one day, something shifts.

The flapping becomes less frantic, the landings less chaotic. The young raven starts to feel its wings—not just as awkward limbs that flail about, but as the source of its ability to explore further than it may have thought possible. It catches the wind and rides it higher than the branches, higher than the treetops.

The same bird that once struggled to stay upright now soars with purpose, exploring a world that was always waiting for it.

No longer content to stay close to the ground under the watchful eyes of its parents, the raven sets out further. It soars, gliding over the forest canopy, over the tumultuous waters of rivers below, over deep canyons and valleys. It doesn't question whether its wings can support it.

It knows.

And because it knows, the possibilities of what it can do and where it can go are endless.

Which means, it starts to play.

Performing rolls, somersaults, and even flying upside down. *Yeah, they can fly upside down.* With their wings fully stretched and their confidence soaring, they don't just fly—they experiment. They embrace the air in ways most other birds never will, flipping their perspective and testing their limits.

What once seemed impossible becomes second nature. The raven has learned that its wings aren't just for survival—they're for discovery and joy.

And your wings are no different.

So, think about how far you've already come. Take a minute to flip through your journal and look at your notes. Read the reminders taped to your mirror. And while you're there look at yourself and smile.

*Really.*

Go back and see how much clearer your own strengths and abilities are now. How you see yourself differently. How the person in the mirror has grown in their resolve.

Buying this book was your first leap. Every chapter since has helped you recover what was lost, reconnect with your values, and begin crafting the life you forgot you wanted, step-by-step.

*Or with every flap.*

The nest—your comfort zone—has served its purpose. It gave you safety so you could learn and experiment. But staying there too long doesn't rescue your dreams. It lets them suffocate. So, now you have to trust your wings.

And what are your wings for?

They're for flying, soaring, and even playing.

But most importantly, they're for answering the vital question: **Where are you going?**

---

## BAD THINGS GROW IN A COMFORT ZONE

---

If answering "Where are you going?" makes you uncomfortable, you're not alone.

The thought of steering your life toward a destination you've never been before can feel overwhelming. Which is why the second we take a meaningful step toward the life we want, many of us want to scream, **"I'M OUT OF MY COMFORT ZONE!"**

Which can convince you that you're running blindly into some scary, unknown place without a map, a light, or a lifeline.

But that's not how it works.

See, you're never completely out of your comfort zone. You're always expanding it, stretching it, and growing it. Because what's really happening is that in every new endeavor, you bring with you your experience, your knowledge, and your values. Which are some of your greatest comforts.

Just think of all the tools you've gained throughout this book—clarity, boundaries, vulnerability, connection. Those comforting tools don't stay rooted in place when you venture out and try new things; they come with you into every new challenge.

But the more you tell yourself you're out of your comfort zone, the more fear and a sense of inadequacy grow, whispering that you're not ready, that you can't handle what's ahead.

Courage shrinks under that kind of narrative.

Sometimes, that feeling of "comfort" is simply fear growing in disguise, showing up as the warmest, coziest blanket. It feels good, safe, and even rational. But if you stay wrapped in it too long, you risk turning your comfort zone into a shallow grave where your dreams are buried.

And fear isn't the only thing that grows in a comfort zone. For some people, it's their misery, complaints, pessimism, and even their unhappiness.

*Does that hit a nerve?*

There's another danger of not expanding your comfort zone: The longer you stay there, the harder it becomes to grow your baseline for happiness. I mean, how long until you're bored, discontent, or unmotivated because you think what you've experienced is all that you can handle?

That's why it's so important to expand your comfort zone. Doing so reminds you that the world is a big, beautiful place, full of possibilities—not a small, dark corner where you quietly settle for less.

So, just like in Chapter 1, it's time to reframe the story you're telling yourself. Instead of saying, **"I'm out of my comfort zone"** try:

- **I'm stretching my comfort zone.**
- **I'm growing my comfort zone.**
- **I'm expanding my comfort zone.**

All of those are true. Stretching reminds you that growth is happening, and that your world is expanding. And more importantly, that your values and resolve for the life you want should always speak louder than your fears.

With that mindset, courage doesn't shrink—it grows.

And even your brain will thank you for the new adventures.

Because stretching your comfort zone doesn't just build your courage—it rewires your brain to crave growth. Every time you try something new and exciting, your brain releases dopamine—the chemical that makes you feel rewarded and energized. It's the same reason refreshing your social media feed is so satisfying: your brain is hooked on discovery.

And one of the things you'll discover, as you stretch and grow, is a new relationship with fear—our scary but necessary riding companion.

## WHAT ARE YOU SO SCARED OF?

I'm fascinated by fear.

Because there's no other emotion like it that will instantly put life into perspective for you.

For example, if you have a health scare, you instantly value what you may have taken for granted: time with loved ones, the ability to move your body, your independence, the hope of another day—even the ability to dream of better days and build the life you want.

Just like that, fear has a way of sobering you up to what's really important.

Fear often shows up in life's bigger moments—like that health scare, or when you're about to step into something completely new, maybe take a leap toward a bold vision, or when you begin to challenge everything you've ever known and believed in. These are the times when fear shouts the loudest, trying to convince you to stay where it feels safe.

But fear also whispers in the quieter moments. It's there when you hesitate to speak up in a meeting, try something unfamiliar, or set a boundary for the very first time. These smaller moments may feel less dramatic, but they're just as important. They're where you practice leaning into discomfort, testing your courage, and preparing for the bigger leaps ahead.

And this is why fear matters—when channeled well, it can be one of your greatest allies.

Healthy fear keeps you safe. It stops you from doing something reckless—like sticking your hand in a fire or walking blindly into danger. But healthy fear doesn't just protect you. It can also guide you. When you're stepping into the unknown, fear is a signal that you're on the edge of something meaningful. It's saying, *This matters to you.*

I know that may sound strange, but take a moment to reflect on this: When was the last time fear rose up in your life?

Maybe it was before giving a big presentation, sharing an idea you deeply believed in, or having a vulnerable conversation with someone you care about. That fear wasn't random—it was there because the stakes were high.

Fear points to the moments where you care enough to risk failure, rejection, or discomfort.

And isn't that what growth requires? Something that matters enough to you, that you'd be willing to muster your courage and move forward in spite of your fear?

I'm tired of hearing this permeating message that encourages us to be "fearless", as if that's something to brag about. Like fear is the big, bad, villain in your life and you have to vanquish it.

That's ridiculous.

You need your fear to stay protected and in order to grow. Healthy fear can push you to stretch beyond what's comfortable, to challenge yourself, and to step into something bigger.

It's not the enemy.

Imagine a musician stepping onto a stage for the first time. Fear is there, in the shaky hands and pounding heart. But as they play, they grow more confident, and with every performance, their comfort zone expands.

The same is true for you. Fear can show up when you're at the edge of something meaningful and great:

- **Starting a new job.**
- **Launching a dream project.**
- **Setting boundaries for the first time.**
- **Committing to a relationship—or ending one that's no longer serving you.**

In those moments, fear isn't there to stop you. It's there to remind you that you're stepping into territory that matters. It's a guide, a compass pointing to the areas where your courage is needed and where the next chapter of your story begins.

But for fear to guide you, you need to understand it. Because unhealthy fear thrives in uncertainty. If you don't get clear about what you're really afraid of, it can grow into a huge, poisonous monster, leaving you paralyzed.

Thankfully, illumination is your antidote.

## DID YOU HEAR THAT?

No one fears the darkness itself.

What scares us is what might be in the darkness—the thing that goes bump in the night, the unseen phantom, the imagined threats lurking beyond what we can perceive.

And that distinction is everything.

This is why illumination is so important. Without having that clarity, fear becomes a vague, shadowy force you can't name or face. It leaves you directionless because how do you fight or tame something you can't define?

So, when it comes to going after the life you really want, what's the thing that really goes bump in the night for you?

Failing?

Getting hurt?

Looking foolish?

When you specifically name your fear, you can set goals that help you move through it, weaken its grip, and even harness it.

Take glossophobia, for example—the fear of public speaking.

Approximately 75% of people in the United States are scared to get up and speak in front of an audience. It's easy to assume they all share the same fear.

But they don't.

And as long as it's generalized as simply "being scared to speak in public," the real monsters in the dark go unaddressed.

Some people are self-conscious about how they look, and that insecurity fuels their fear of standing in front of others.

Others fear stumbling over their words and being laughed at.

And some? They're totally fine with the audience laughing—as long as they feel confident in what they're saying.

See, by being more specific—by naming the fear (self-conscious about appearance, fear of ridicule, lack of confidence)—they can target and address those exact concerns. And when they do that, they can set goals to eliminate or at least mitigate them.

They can wear clothes that make them feel attractive.

Rehearse what they want to say.

Do more research to feel more prepared.

Naming your fears allows you to manage them instead of letting them manage you.

Clarity turns fear from a shadowy unknown into something you can confront, understand, and even use. The goal is not always to eliminate fear. The goal is to be scared, and if it means enough to you, do it anyway. Channel it. Grow from it. And allow the fear to diminish.

Fear does not have to be a stop sign; it can be a forge. And with the right tools, fear can become the thing that builds and galvanizes your courage.

## FIGHT, FLIGHT, FREEZE, OR FAWN?

We often talk about fight or flight as automatic reactions to fear.

And some of you might also know about freeze—or even fawn.

These fearful reactions are instinctive and can feel like they're beyond our control. In a lot of ways our brains are still looking for the big, bad, T-Rex that just might want you for lunch. And when that happens, fear can hijack your body and mind, sending you into a spiral of uncontrollable reactivity—and often, regret.

But we really don't have to worry about that T-Rex anymore. And many times, you *can* control your fears. And with the right mindset, every one of them can be a tool for growth.

Because when you understand and harness them, these fearful reactions become courageous responses that have the potential to help you move forward, in spite of feeling afraid.

Here's what these fearful reactions often look like—and how you can reframe them into courageous responses for intentional action:

### FIGHT

### Out of Control: The Reaction to Lash Out

- Reacting with defensiveness or aggression, lashing out to protect yourself.

- Believing that attacking is the only way to stay safe.

### In Control: The Courage to Stand Your Ground

- Standing up for your boundaries and values with assertiveness.

- **Ask yourself:** What am I willing to stand up for, even when it's hard?

- **Example:** Advocating for yourself calmly in a difficult conversation.

## FLIGHT

### Out of Control: The Reaction to Flee

- Avoiding challenges entirely, running away from risks and opportunities that scare you.

- *"It's easier to quit than to try and possibly fail."*

### In Control: The Courage to Change Direction

- Choosing to leave situations that no longer serve you, aligning your actions with your vision.

- **Ask yourself:** Is this fear pointing to something I need to change to protect my dreams?

- **Example:** Walking away from a toxic job or relationship to pursue something healthier.

## FREEZE

### Out of Control: The Reaction to Shut Down

- Feeling paralyzed, unable to act or make a decision.

- *"Do nothing, say nothing, be nothing—it's too dangerous."*

### In Control: The Courage to Pause and Reflect

• Using stillness as an opportunity to gather clarity and focus before taking deliberate action.

• **Ask yourself:** What's the smallest step I can take to break through this stillness?

• **Example:** Taking a breath, reflecting on your next step, and starting small.

### FAWN

### Out of Control: The Reaction to Please

• People-pleasing to avoid rejection or conflict, sacrificing your own needs to keep others happy.

• *"You have to say yes, or they'll stop caring about you."*

### In Control: The Courage to Honor Yourself

• Self-care, setting boundaries and prioritizing what strengthens you, rather than overextending yourself.

• **Ask yourself:** What strengths do I have that can help me honor *my* needs and values?

• **Example:** Putting yourself first by saying no to demands that drain you and instead creating space for what truly matters to you.

So, the next time you feel afraid, take an intentional pause and ask yourself:

• **What is the thing I'm really scared of? Name it.**

• **Which of the four fears am I feeling?**

- **Is this fear trying to protect me or reminding me how much this matters?**

- **How can I turn this fearful reaction into a courageous response that aligns with my goals and values?**

Remember, fear doesn't have to control you—it can empower you.

By recognizing and reframing your fear reactions, you can turn what once felt out of control into intentional tools for growth.

Because the truth is, your wings aren't made of fear—they're made of courage.

---

## I BELIEVE IT'S TIME FOR ME TO FLY

---

And by *me*, I mean *you*.

Because like the raven, it's time to trust the courage of your wings to take you farther, higher, and more confidently into new horizons.

So, let's review.

At the end of Part 1, you had a "stand and deliver" moment when you answered the question, *"Who are you?"* And this was all about your core sense of self—your identity. And how your *being* should inform your *doing*.

I shared my answer: *"I'm sunlight."*

That's my identity and it informs everything I do, every choice I make, every direction I head in. And although I'm not always successful, it's a powerful guiding framework in my life.

My hope for you is that your answer to *"Who are you?"* has been guiding you with a greater sense of intention and truth as well.

Knowing that living at full choice, from your values, is empowering you to save the life you forgot you wanted. Or maybe didn't even know was waiting for you.

Now, as we near the end of this chapter and Part 2 of this guidebook, it's time to answer the next vital question, **Where are you going?**

What's the direction you're headed in—your focus—your goal? Meaning, what is it that you'll be *doing*, that is informed by who you are—your *being*.

In Chapter 4 you began mapping out where you wanted to go, and along with it, you identified milestones that you needed to reach, helped by your SMART goals, in order to rescue your dreams.

Look back at your journal, how did you articulate that sense of direction? Did you make a list of things you'd like to accomplish? Have? Resolve? Did you discover some monster needs that had been derailing you? Some boundaries that needed to be put up? Some connections you needed to nurture and grow? And some fears to use as fuel?

The answers to all of those things should have brought some tremendous clarity to your life and your vision, along with some traction that will finally get you out of that pit and spreading your wings to fly.

Once you reach your goals and stand triumphantly on your accomplishments, what is it that you'll continue to be doing—that you should have been, or even could have been doing all along? What's the thing you're made to do, that keeps driving you in a focused direction every single day?

**"[I'm going to]** ... *illuminate the dark corners of people's lives so they can see what's keeping them anchored in place—so they know what's been holding them back from the life they forgot they wanted to live."*

That's where *I'm* going and it's what I'm doing, every single day.

Because sunlight doesn't stay still. It stretches, it expands, it reaches into every shadow to bring light, warmth, and clarity. It has direction, focus, and a goal.

---

## WHERE ARE YOU GOING?

---

Open your journal.

On a fresh page at the top write, **Where are you going?**

Then write, **I am going ...**

Remember, when you answer *Where are you going?* you're not just describing a destination. You're describing the kind of life you're building.

Your goals—whether they're about your career, relationships, or personal growth—are part of this, but they're not the whole story.

This question asks you to step back and see the bigger picture. It invites you to name the world you're creating for yourself and the people around you.

Based on the vision for your life that you refined in Chapter 4, and in spite of the challenges of needs, boundaries, connections, and fear, answer the question in a way that summarizes the big picture for you. Not just the individual goals. Not just the elements of the dream life. But the totality of your identity in action.

**Ask yourself:**

- **What kind of life do I want to create?**
- **What kind of impact do I want to have?**
- **How does my identity influence the path I'm taking?**

I know that this can feel so challenging to articulate, because we're conditioned to not talk too much about ourselves unless we get accused of bragging or not being humble.

And it can feel uncomfortable to not just say it, but to believe you're the right person to go and do what you dream of.

Your answer doesn't have to be something that the world considers grand and notable. It just has to be meaningful to you and *your* world.

No matter big or small it may seem to others.

Now, it's natural to hear 'Where are you going?' and think of a location—a place you'll arrive at one day. But that's not what this question is *really* asking.

The truth is, your actions, choices, and commitments *create* the destination. Every step you take moves you in a direction, shaping the world you will eventually arrive in.

In the examples below, you'll notice a pattern—each answer starts with **I'm GOING TO...** That's because you're defining what you're going to do that creates where you'll end up.

Here are some good examples that may resonate with you:

**Creative & Personal Fulfillment**

- I'm going to create art that sparks emotion and connects with people on a deeper level, reminding them of the beauty in the world.

- I'm going to master my craft, whether that's baking, coding, or carpentry, and find joy in the process of getting better every day.

- I'm going to write stories that help others see themselves in a new light and feel less alone in the world.

## Advocacy & Social Impact

- I'm going to fight for the rights of the underrepresented, ensuring their voices are heard and their stories are told.

- I'm going to champion mental health, breaking stigmas and creating spaces for healing and understanding.

- I'm going to advocate for change, helping shape a world where equality and justice are not just ideals, but realities.

## Family & Community Building

- I'm going to be a great parent, raising children who feel loved, supported, and empowered to create their own meaningful paths in life.

- I'm going to grow a garden that nourishes not just my family but my neighbors, building a small, sustainable way to give back to my community.

- I'm going to start a business that serves my community, offering something of real value and creating opportunities for others to thrive.

## Connection & Relationships

- I'm going to foster a safe space for others, where they can feel heard, valued, and encouraged to grow.

- I'm going to build meaningful relationships, showing up for the people I care about and fostering connections that matter.

- I'm going to inspire my community by building bridges between people who think they have nothing in common.

## Self-Growth & Resilience

- I'm going to run my first marathon, proving to myself that I can set big goals and achieve them step by step.

- I'm going to heal old wounds, forgiving others and myself so I can move forward with peace and strength.

- I'm going to lead by example, showing those around me that it's never too late to grow, change, and create a life that aligns with your values.

## Joy & Sustainability

- I'm going to bring joy to others, through small, everyday moments of kindness, laughter, and connection.

- I'm going to design sustainable solutions, making the world a better place for future generations.

- I'm going to empower people, helping them step into their potential and reclaim their confidence.

Once you've written your answer, look at it closely and ask yourself:

- **Does this feel true?**
- **Does it reflect who I am and the life I want to create?**
- **Does it scare me a little—in the best possible way?**

Once you have your answer go the mirror. *Guess what's coming?*

Out loud, declare your answer to **Who are you?**

Now, out loud declare your answer to **Where are you going?**

Then tear out that sheet of paper and tape it next to the others. Let those pages remind you that you're living at full choice, becoming who you were always meant to be, and on a journey to rescue your dreams.

# SO NOW WHAT?

So, you know who you are.

And now you know where you're going.

Now, let's find out why you're going there.

"What lies behind us and what lies before us are tiny matters compared to what lies within us."

- *Ralph Waldo Emerson*

# PART 3
## WHY ARE YOU GOING THERE?

# WHY ARE YOU GOING THERE?

Let's reminisce.

Part 1 of this guidebook challenged you to uncover who you truly are, taking out the head trash and putting you on a more secure path far from the edges of expectation and cliffs of comparison that kill your identity.

Part 2 pushed you even harder. And I know it was a heavy lift, but it was a necessary one. Refining your vision of the life you dream of, breaking it down into actionable steps, challenging you to meet your needs, finding connection through vulnerability, and spreading your wings.

Now, it's time to connect the dots. To uncover the fire that ignites your dreams and illuminates the path ahead of you no matter how dark it may get.

*Why?*

Because your life is worth it. And because the answer to that question ties everything together.

Why are you here? Why does your life matter? Why keep showing up, doing the hard work, and striving to rescue your dreams?

Because of your purpose.

Purpose is the answer to *Why?* It's the passionate fire that burns within you, lighting the way forward and burning down what no longer serves you. It's what gives clarity to your identity and fuel to your vision.

Without purpose, the work you've done so far risks becoming meaningless. Just one more thing on your "to do" list. But when you start to uncover it? It changes everything.

In the introduction of this book I shared that April 10, 1996, was the darkest night of my life. A night where I couldn't see anything ahead of me—no future, no hope, no reason to keep going. But on April 11th I woke up and something in my spirit had radically shifted.

Something divine reached down and illuminated my soul, and I felt the greatest sense of hope. But surprisingly, I still didn't know my purpose or have all the answers. I only knew that my life had tremendous value and that it was worth taking one more step.

And then the step after that.

That's how fire begins: with a spark.

Over time, and with each step, that fire got bigger and brighter—with my purpose becoming clearer and clearer. To help people rescue their dreams so they can transform their reality.

See, purpose isn't always handed to you in a single, life-altering moment. It's usually uncovered piece by piece through connection—to yourself, to others, and to the world you want to create. It doesn't arrive fully formed, but it grows as you reflect, act, and keep moving forward.

Maybe you've felt that spark for yourself? I hope you have. And I hope that the work you've done through this guidebook has stoked the flames brighter than they've been for you in a long time.

Because unfortunately, most people never find their fire.

They spend their lives chasing distractions, settling for "good enough," or burying their dreams under fear and self-doubt.

But you? You're not most people.

By choosing to do this work, you've proven that you're willing to go where others won't. And because of that, you're closer than ever to saving the life you forgot you wanted.

And who knows, maybe your purpose will ignite a fire in others.

If identity is your foundation and vision is your compass, purpose is the fire that makes it all come alive. It's what keeps you moving forward when the road is hard and the obstacles feel endless. It's the energy that fuels transformation—not just for you, but for everyone you touch.

So, let's go discover your purpose. Because it's time to light the fire within you—and let it blaze a path forward.

# CHAPTER 9

## WHAT'S THE POINT OF PURPOSE?

Purpose is such a big word, isn't it? It feels like a mystical energy or impulse—a magnetic pull toward something bigger.

But what does it truly mean?

The dictionary defines purpose as "the reason for which something is done or created or for which something exists." It's a simple explanation. Eating, drinking, and breathing keep us alive. Sleeping helps us function. Tires exist to make a car move, just as a stovetop exists to cook.

Purpose in the everyday is easy to identify—it's woven into how we interact with the world around us.

Yet the *purpose* for your life seems incredibly challenging to nail down or even articulate. Because your unique purpose is so much more. It's the fire we talked about in the intro of part 3—fueling your identity and vision. It's what keeps you moving when everything else feels like it's trying to stop you.

And to know your purpose and claim it comes with a tremendous sense of personal responsibility to live it out intentionally.

You've felt the stirrings of it before, haven't you?

That subtle yet unmistakable pull during moments when you felt deeply connected to something or someone. It might have been the satisfaction of solving a problem, the quiet joy of being fully present with someone you care about, or the undeniable feeling that your effort or your creation positively affected the world.

Those moments weren't random—they were whispers of your purpose.

Now some of you may already know your purpose and it just got buried along with the rest of your dreams. If that's you, the rest of this guidebook should serve to breathe new life into it.

But for most of you, your purpose is just a whisper or maybe even silent. And that's really okay, because after learning who you are, and where you're going, your purpose is closer than ever to being found. Meaning you already have everything you need to begin.

Purpose isn't waiting for some distant future or a perfect moment— it's been waiting for you to notice it in the life you're already living.

But that doesn't mean finding it is always easy.

Purpose is deeply personal, yet it's never entirely about you. It connects your identity and vision to the world around you. It thrives in relationships, in contribution, in the ripples of impact your life creates. Purpose lives in that intersection between what you care about and the difference you can make.

And you have no purpose outside of connection. Which is why this need must always be met.

Now, even though finding your purpose can be challenging, it's not impossible. You just need to know where to look.

# WHAT DOES PURPOSE LOOK LIKE?

Purpose is found in the everyday moments where your values bloom into your actions and intersects with others. It's felt when you lean into your strengths, pursue what lights you up, and find ways to serve others in meaningful ways.

A great way to understand this is to look toward others who have lived or are living purposeful lives:

### Oprah Winfrey

Oprah's life began in rural Mississippi, marked by poverty and hardship. As a child, she faced abuse, neglect, and the uncertainty of being passed between caregivers. These early challenges could have defined her—but they didn't.

Instead, Oprah found solace in her love for storytelling and connection. She began by speaking into small microphones, dreaming big dreams.

Over time, her purpose revealed itself: to empower, educate, and inspire others by sharing stories that mattered.

Through her shows, books, and philanthropic work, Oprah became a builder of bridges, (and a giver of cars) showing countless people that their stories were worth telling and their lives were worth living.

### Maya Angelou

Maya Angelou endured devastating trauma as a child, which left her mute for nearly five years. In that silence, she found refuge in books and poetry, where her voice began to take shape.

Her purpose became clear as she began to speak—not just with her voice, but with her poetry, autobiographies, and activism. Her words became a light in dark places, helping others reclaim their dignity and their stories.

One of her most profound teachings was, "When you learn, teach. When you get, give."

Maya lived that, lifting others as she rose.

### Fred Rogers

Fred Rogers had a quiet, steady presence that became his gift to the world. He used his show, *Mister Rogers' Neighborhood,* to teach kindness, empathy, and emotional intelligence to children.

And Fred understood the power of small gestures. One of his most famous moments was when he invited François Clemmons, an African American actor who played a postman on the show, to join him in cooling off by soaking their feet together in a small pool.

Fred then gently helped dry François's feet, a simple yet profound act of love and humanity during a time of racial division in America. It showed children what it truly meant to care for one another.

Fred's purpose was rooted in service, proving that the greatest transformations often happen in the smallest moments. And because of it, it was always a beautiful day in the neighborhood.

## HOW DOES IT SHOW UP?

It's inspiring to hear about people like Oprah, Maya, and Fred, whose lives seem larger than our own. But purpose isn't reserved for public figures or grand gestures. It's alive in the everyday moments where someone's presence or actions make the world a little better without fanfare:

- **Purpose shows up in the teacher who stays after class, making sure no student feels left behind.**

- **It's in the barista who learns your name and remembers your order, brightening your morning with a kind word and a smile.**

- **It's in the friend who always seems to know when to call, somehow sensing that you need them before you even realize it yourself.**

These people may not even realize the impact they're having. They might brush it off and say, "Oh, I was just being me," or "It was nothing." But with purpose, it's always something.

I've seen a quote that says:

**"Some of you are walking 'love letters' and you don't even realize it. You're lighting up rooms, shifting atmospheres, and carrying inspiration just by being you. Such a precious gift."**

Such a precious gift is right. Count yourself as lucky—blessed even, if you have just one person in your life like that.

As a matter of fact, let's pause for a moment.

Think about the people in your life who have made a difference. Maybe it's a friend who checked in at just the right moment, or a mentor whose encouragement changed how you saw yourself. Perhaps it's someone whose small, consistent kindness has quietly brightened your days.

Pick someone and send them an encouraging text.

*Right now.*

Don't just say thank you—tell them why.

Be specific.

Let them know how their actions, their presence, or simply who they are has impacted you in a positive way.

**It could be as simple as:**

- "Your advice last year gave me the clarity I needed to move forward. I can't thank you enough for being there when I needed it most."

- "Every time we talk, you make me feel seen and valued. I don't know if I've ever told you, but it means the world to me. Thank you for being you!"

- "You've always believed in me, even when I doubted myself. Your encouragement gave me the confidence to take the leap I was so afraid of. I'll never forget what that meant to me—thank you."

And if you're feeling bold, I'll give you 500 bonus points for calling some of them instead of texting. There's something about hearing gratitude spoken aloud that carries even more weight.

Purpose doesn't need permission to shine. It will express itself through your values and actions, whether or not you recognize it.

---

## REVISITING YOUR VALUES

---

In Chapter 3 you identified your core values—the principles that guide your life, the ones that reflect the best of who you are.

Take a moment to look back at what you wrote then. Grab your journal and read those values out loud. Start each one with, **"I value …"**

Now, take it further. After each value, say why you value it.

Speak the words, even if it feels awkward at first. Let yourself hear the meaning behind what matters to you.

**For example:**

- "**I value kindness** because it creates connection and trust in my relationships."

- "**I value creativity** because it lets me express myself and inspire others."

- "**I value perseverance** because it reminds me I can overcome anything."

Your values are the threads that weave your purpose. Saying them out loud allows you to fully embody them and remind yourself of how they show up in your life. Which should help bring your purpose into focus more, even if it's still a bit blurry.

Now, let's take this reflection a little further.

I want to ask you two simple but powerful questions—ones that might hold surprising clues about your purpose.

The first question is: **What makes it a great day?**

If you don't know the answer, great days might feel like random blessings, moments you stumble into by chance.

But if you do know, you can start to move through your life with intention. You can recognize the people, actions, and experiences that create joy and fulfillment and make space for more of them.

Somewhere in that answer—what makes it a great day for you—lie the seeds of your purpose.

Think about it. Living in your purpose lights you up. That's why fire and passion are such important images when we talk about purpose. Purpose ignites something inside you—it energizes you, fuels you, and gives you life.

So, open your journal and make the time to answer—what makes it a great day for you?

Maybe it's volunteering your time to help someone in need, whether it's lending a hand to a neighbor, mentoring a student, or contributing to a cause you care deeply about. Purpose might be showing you *why* those moments of service matter—not just in the way they reflect your values, but how it helps those who need it, and inspires others to do the same.

Or maybe it's finally finishing something you've been working on for weeks, where you feel a surge of pride and accomplishment. In that, purpose might be telling you *why* perseverance matters—not just for your growth, but to show others that effort creates value, and creating as much as you consume makes the world richer for everyone.

Or maybe it's having a deep conversation with someone who really gets you, where you walk away feeling seen, heard, and valued. Purpose could be showing you *why* those connections are vital—not just for your own heart but for the mutual trust and support they bring into both of your lives.

Whatever it is, those moments aren't random. They're quietly pointing you toward what matters most.

Now, the second question: **What makes it a bad day?**

If you don't know the answer, bad days will keep blindsiding you.

The storm clouds will gather, the ground will shift beneath you, and suddenly you'll find yourself wondering what happened.

But when you understand what makes it a bad day, you can start to recognize the signs. You might not always avoid it, but you can prepare yourself.

And often, those bad days feel so heavy because they pull you away from your purpose.

Maybe a bad day is when you feel unproductive, like you've wasted your energy on things that don't really matter. Purpose might be nudging you *why* that feels so wrong—reminding you that your time is best spent where it can create meaning, both for you and the people you serve.

Or maybe it's when you're stretched too thin, saying yes to too many things that drain your energy. Purpose might be showing you *why* your boundaries are important—not just to protect yourself but to ensure you can show up fully for the things and people who matter most.

Or maybe it's when you've spent the whole day on tasks or with people who feel completely out of sync with your values. Purpose might be waving a red flag, reminding you *why* intention matters—to avoid the moments that drain you so you can invest in those that fill you and others up.

See, reflecting on your values and exploring the patterns in your great days and bad days gives you a glimpse into the story your purpose is trying to tell.

These insights—guideposts, are pointing you toward the things that light you up and the moments that pull you off course.

All in an effort to ensure that your purpose is always leading the way.

Let's go further ...

# MY WHY

At the beginning of Part 3 I mentioned that my purpose wasn't something I uncovered all at once. It unfolded gradually as I reflected, connected, and took consistent and meaningful action in my life. Until those whispers of my spirit became a passionate cry that I could no longer ignore.

As I've shared, April 11, 1996, was a whole new beginning for me. But let me be clear—I didn't wake up with all my problems solved. The problems still existed, I just saw my ability to move through them and learn from them differently.

It was as if the darkness that had clouded my life had lifted, and for the first time, I saw color. The world wasn't a shadow anymore—it felt alive. I could hear the wind whispering through the leaves, and everything seemed to pulse with vibrant energy. For the first time, I took a breath that didn't feel weighed down—it felt light, like it was filled with hope.

Possibility. That's what it felt like.

And I believe something much bigger than me stepped in that day and planted a seed. A calling. A purpose. Now my job was to discover it.

- **Why** did I go into prisons in Chicago to minister to those behind bars?

- **Why** did I sit with the homeless in Toronto, listening to their stories and getting to know their struggles?

- **Why** did I mentor under-resourced youth, helping them see their own greatness?

- **Why** did I deliver keynote speeches on leadership?

- **Why** did I work with corporate teams to unlock their potential?

- **Why** did I dedicate myself to growing my understanding of human development and potential?

- **Why** did I write this book?

Because everything I was doing came back to one focused purpose: to help Rescue Your Dreams.

At the time, I didn't fully understand the deeper "why" behind those choices. I just kept waking up each day and moving forward.

My sense of purpose grew slowly, year by year, as I realized my life wasn't meant to end. It was meant to help others see what they couldn't—to illuminate the dark corners of their lives where insecurity, doubt, and fear kept them anchored. To show them how to cut those anchors loose and move toward the dreams they thought were out of reach.

See, purpose connects everything you do with meaning. It turns what might look like separate threads into a unified story.

And when you find your "why," it changes the way you see yourself, your work, and your relationships.

---

## UNCOVERING YOUR WHY

---

When you think about the moments in your life that mattered most, patterns begin to emerge. These are the times when your purpose quietly revealed itself—through the things you value, the strengths you bring to the table, and the connections you create with others.

Now, it's your turn to uncover those patterns.

Get out your journal and see what you can discover by answering these questions:

- **When have you felt most alive?**

  Think about a moment when your world seemed to hum with energy.

  Maybe it was standing in front of a crowd, the sound of applause echoing in your ears, their admiration fueling the rhythm of your heartbeat.

  Maybe it was the rush of adrenaline as you leapt into the unknown—traveling somewhere new, chasing an adventure, or saying yes to an opportunity that stretched you.

  Or maybe it was a quiet moment, the kind that feels electric because you were completely present, fully engaged, and fully you.

- **When have you felt at your strongest—mentally, emotionally, physically, or spiritually?**

  Picture a time when you felt unshakable.

  Maybe it was climbing a literal or metaphorical mountain, pushing through exhaustion to prove to yourself what you're capable of.

  Maybe it was a moment of resolve, standing firm in your beliefs or protecting someone you love.

  Or perhaps it was a time when you felt untouchable, when every step you took seemed to clear the path ahead of you, and you knew you could conquer anything that came your way.

  Let those questions marinate. You don't have to take them off the burner yet. They're a slow simmer, allowing you to deeply reflect on the things that matter most.

- **Ask Trusted Voices**

Sometimes, purpose is hard to see from the inside. The people who know us best can often spot patterns and strengths we might miss, even shedding light on the impact we've had on others—which is why connection is so vital to this process.

Here's where you ask for their insight:

- **When have you seen me at my best?**

- **What strengths do you think I bring into a room or a relationship?**

- **How do you think I positively impact others?**

Imagine a friend telling you, "You light up every time you talk about mentoring your students," or "Your ability to stay calm under pressure inspires everyone around you." These reflections can reveal aspects of your purpose you hadn't recognized.

As you listen to their responses, resist the urge to dismiss compliments or downplay your impact. Trust that the people you're asking see something real in you. Write their words down and notice any recurring themes—they're like puzzle pieces helping you build a clearer picture of your "why."

**Now tie it all together and look for the patterns.**

Take everything you've uncovered—your reflections on when you felt alive and strong, and the insights from trusted voices—and sit with this final question:

**What do these moments reveal about the direction my life is pulling me toward?**

Your purpose already exists in the self-enhancing patterns of your life, waiting to be uncovered. It's in the energy that keeps pulling you forward, the themes that keep repeating, and the connections that light the way.

**"The two most important days in your life are the day you are born and the day you find out why."**

*- Mark Twain*

That *"why"* is your purpose. And it's far more than a title, an achievement, or the tasks you complete in a day. Purpose is a force—a fire—that makes your life bigger than the sum of its parts.

Purpose is something you carry with you and express in everything you do. It's not static—it grows, shifts, and deepens as you move through life. It's what gives your actions meaning and creates ripples in the lives of others.

And you will be fulfilling it until your last breath.

---

## SO NOW WHAT?

---

Now, I'm sure you were hoping this would be the moment your purpose revealed itself, tied up neatly with a bow and a dramatic journal entry.

But we're not done yet. Because before you can fully uncover it, we need to summon your warhorses: Resilience and Grit. These are the steeds that will make your purpose unstoppable.

Let's finish what we started.

# CHAPTER 10

## HOW BAD DO YOU WANT IT?

Every journey has a moment when the excitement fades, the novelty wears off, and you really feel the grind.

Which is when your steps forward can feel incredibly heavy.

It's the part of the journey that tests you, stretches you, and shapes you. And it's where most people stop—not because they didn't care, but because the work felt too hard.

And truth be told, maybe they didn't care as much as they thought they did.

Which means they go back to the same patterns—the ones you may have had when you first cracked open this book. The patterns that keep people on a squeaky, run-down, treadmill of self-defeating behaviors and unhappiness.

But you're still here, because you made a promise to yourself back in the introduction.

And since you can never say it enough, flip open to the first page of your journal again and read what you wrote out loud:

**I'm committed to doing the work necessary for meaningful change in my life.**

Now here we are in the last official chapter of the book. My hope is that every step of the way, you've honored yourself by keeping that promise—even if it meant working through a few ugly cries in the process.

Hard work isn't glamorous and it's usually messy. And because big dreams require the long game, the journey rarely feels rewarding in the moment; like writing another page when the words won't come, showing up to the gym when your bed is so comfortable, or maybe even having an honest conversation when silence feels safer.

It's like planting seeds. You bury them in the soil, water them, and tend to them, even when you can't see what's happening beneath the surface. You trust the process. You trust that all the effort—the daily choices to keep going—will lead to growth.

But trusting the process doesn't mean the work is easy. The hard work asks for patience and requires consistency. It demands that you show up again and again, even when progress feels distant.

This is where your resilience is strengthened, your grit is tested, and your resolve is grown.

And no matter how weak you may feel in those areas, you will always build their capacity every time you choose to do the hard work. Every time you show up, these tools get stronger—increasing your determination.

And you need these tools to rescue your dreams. Because without them, some challenges will just be too heavy to carry.

Executing the difficult tasks with consistency will test what you're willing to fight for. It will reveal how bad you want it, and how strong your sense of purpose is.

Meaning, it will force you to answer, what are you *really* willing to fight for?

And that answer won't always be what you expect.

Personally, I think wealth is nice. Applause feels good. Recognition and toys are fun. But I'm not willing to go into battle for those things. If you are, that's great. Keep on the path that matters most to you. But for me, I'm not willing to die on the sword for those things.

What matters most to me is helping you rescue your dreams.

That's what I'll fight for every day.

The same process applies to you. The hard work will refine you, test you. It will sift through what you think you want, leaving behind the things that are personally most important. The things you can't live without.

This is what your commitment has been about, discovering what's worth the work.

And that discovery?

That's what transforms your reality.

---

## RESILIENCE

---

Resilience is defined as "the ability to recover quickly from setbacks" (*Oxford English Dictionary*). But it's more than a definition. It's a lifeline.

Think of resilience as the pits, holes, and obstacles you encounter along your journey. They trip you up when you least expect it. Maybe you lose your footing entirely and fall into a hole so deep, it feels impossible to climb out. You sit there for a moment, staring at the walls around you, scraped, bruised, maybe even broken.

But then something stirs inside you.

You rise.

Because the reason *why* you're going to *where* you're going is bigger than any scraped knee or broken leg.

Resilience is the choice to climb out of that hole, dust yourself off, and take the next step—even if it hurts. It's what allows you to keep moving forward, even when the weight of the journey feels unbearable. You will fall. You will struggle. But resilience is what gets you back on your feet, no matter how many times it takes.

J.K. Rowling's story is a powerful example of real-life resilience.

She didn't become the global phenomenon behind Harry Potter without facing incredible hardship.

The idea for *Harry Potter* came to her during a train ride in 1990. Over the next five years, she developed the story, scribbling notes on scraps of paper whenever inspiration struck. It was a labor of love, built in moments stolen from the chaos of life.

But life wasn't kind to her.

Her mother passed away that same year, a devastating loss that shaped her writing in ways she couldn't have imagined. Themes of loss and death became central to the story she was creating. Seeking a fresh start, she moved to Portugal to teach English, where she married and gave birth to her daughter, Jessica.

The marriage didn't last. Rowling returned to the UK as a single mother, struggling to make ends meet. Living in Edinburgh and relying on government assistance, she found moments of refuge in her writing. Cafes became her creative sanctuary—her daughter asleep beside her as she poured everything she had into her manuscript.

She sent it to publishers. And was rejected.

**Twelve times.**

Most people would have stopped.

But she didn't.

Rowling reframed every rejection as a step closer to success. She believed in her story, even when no one else seemed to. Finally, Bloomsbury Publishing saw the potential and took a chance on her work. In 1997, *Harry Potter and the Philosopher's Stone* hit shelves and changed the literary world forever.

The rest is history.

---

## THINK-FEEL-DO

---

I'd love to know the thoughts J.K. Rowling had that kept her going when the world around her seemed to be falling apart.

What was she telling herself when her bank account was empty, when another rejection letter came, or when she wondered if anyone would ever believe in her story?

She's a perfect example of what I mentioned in Chapter 1: *what you think affects how you feel.* And how you feel drives what you do—or sometimes, what you don't do.

So many people live their lives reacting solely to how they feel in the moment. They let those challenging feelings take the wheel, steering their actions without ever stopping to think about what's actually fueling them.

They miss the opportunity to take control of the thoughts driving those feelings. And as a result, they miss the chance to create behaviors that empower them—the kind of behaviors that help you act with intention, with purpose, with full ownership of your life.

Take a moment and really listen to the people around you. Pay attention to how they talk about what they want to do—or what's stopping them:

"Oh, I don't **feel** like doing this right now."

"I **feel** so stupid."

"I **feel** like I'll never be as good as everyone else."

*Sound familiar?*

Maybe you've even caught yourself saying these things. Those words—those stories—have a way of creeping into your thoughts, steering your actions, and keeping you stuck.

And that inaction has a huge cost to your life—one you might not even notice right away. It slowly chips away at your confidence, your progress, and your belief in what's possible. Usually at the expense of settling for less than you deserve, giving up, or even worse—going back to the same patterns that left you miserable to begin with.

See, the thing about resilience is that it starts in the mind.

**"The mind adapts and converts to its own purposes the obstacle to our acting. The impediment to action advances action. What stands in the way becomes the way."**

*- Marcus Aurelius*

This quote is so powerful because Marcus Aurelius doesn't see obstacles as roadblocks. Instead, he reframes them as the way forward.

He could've easily thought, "Well, this must mean I'm not on the right path." But instead, with almost a defiant confidence, he affirmed, "The obstacle is the way."

Now let's show you how much bigger your toolkit for life is by revisiting what we talked about in Chapter 1: the power of flipping the script.

When we first talked about this mindset tool, it was about catching those limiting beliefs—your "head trash"—and turning them into something that works for you. Now, let's build on that foundation and strengthen how you handle challenges by training your mind to see them as opportunities for growth.

Resilience, after all, is about how you think about the challenges you face. And when it comes to mistakes, your mindset makes all the difference.

Reflect on these examples of mindsets when it comes to mistakes and see which one resonates with you:

1. **Mistakes mean I've failed and proved myself unsuccessful.**

2. **Mistakes might happen, and they'll show how unskilled I am.**

3. **Mistakes will show me what doesn't work.**

4. **Mistakes help me learn, grow, and move forward more proficiently.**

The beliefs of examples 1 and 2 will keep you stuck, hesitant, or even afraid to take action. They turn mistakes into a reason to quit.

But shifting to the mindsets in examples 3 and 4 changes everything.

With mindset 3, mistakes become useful feedback. And when you move to mindset 4, you begin to see mistakes as part of the process—a way to grow stronger and more capable over time.

Let's put this into practice. Think about a mistake or challenge you may be holding onto right now.

What story have you been telling yourself about it?

Grab your journal and write it down. Next to it, write which mindset—1, 2, 3, or 4—you've been operating from.

Then ask yourself:

- **What story have I been telling myself about this challenge?**

- **How can I rewrite this story to see the obstacle as the way forward?**

For example: "This mistake proves I'm not good enough" becomes "This mistake is teaching me the skills I need to improve."

Or "This challenge is too big for me" becomes "This challenge is helping me grow into someone who can handle more."

Every time you rewrite these stories, you're building resilience. You're shifting the way you think, feel, and act when things get hard.

## AS EASY AS ABC

I understand that reframing your mindset isn't always easy. Sometimes, the mistakes, challenges, or negative narratives you face feel overwhelming, like they're too big to overcome.

And when that happens, it can compromise your ability to rise—to stay resilient.

This is where a powerful system, developed by psychologist Albert Ellis, can make all the difference. Known as the ABCDE technique, it's a cornerstone of Rational Emotive Behavior Therapy (REBT). It's designed to help you break down the story you're telling yourself, challenge it, and rebuild it into something true and empowering.

Let's look at how to use this system with something we've all faced in life: rejection.

Imagine you've just been turned down for a promotion you really wanted at work. You'd put in the effort, felt confident about your chances, and hoped this would be the next step in your career. But instead, you were passed over.

It stings.

The disappointment feels heavy, and the narrative starts forming in your mind: *"I'm not good enough; I'll never move forward."*

This is where the ABCDE technique steps in. By moving step by step through your ABCs, you can challenge the mindset that's holding you back and reshape it into something that serves you.

### A – Activating Event

This is the triggering event that started the whole narrative. What happened to make you feel this way?

In this case, it's the rejection for the promotion. That's the event that sparked the thought, **I'm not good enough.**

## B – Belief About the Event

This is the actual story you've created about the activating event. What belief are you attaching to the situation?

For this example, the belief might be: **I'm not good enough; I'll never move forward in my career.**

Notice how this belief turns the event into something deeply personal and permanent.

## C – Consequences of That Belief

Your belief has consequences because what you think affects how you feel, and how you feel drives what you do.

Ask yourself: **What are the emotional and behavioral outcomes of this belief?**

If you believe you're not good enough, you might feel inadequate, stuck, or hopeless. Those feelings could lead to avoiding new opportunities, withdrawing, or giving up entirely.

It's critical to recognize that these consequences aren't caused by the rejection itself—they're caused by your belief about the rejection.

## D – Debate the Belief

Now it's time to challenge the story you've created.

**Ask yourself:**

- **Is this belief true?**
- **What evidence contradicts it?**

For instance, you might realize:

- **You've received praise for your work in the past.**

- **You've successfully handled challenges before.**
- **The rejection could be situational—it might have nothing to do with your abilities.**

By poking holes in the negative belief, you start to see it for what it is: just a story, not a fact.

### E – Examine What's Changed

Finally, rewrite the story into something true and empowering.

Instead of: **I'm not good enough; I'll never move forward.**

Your new belief might be: **This rejection is temporary. It's an opportunity to grow, improve, and prepare for the next step in my career.**

Notice how this shift doesn't deny the difficulty of the event—it reframes it into something actionable.

**And Remember:**

As we discussed in Chapter 2, optimism views challenges as:

- **Temporary**, not permanent.
- **Situational**, not pervasive.
- **Not personal**—they're not a reflection of your worth.

When you keep these truths in mind, rewriting your story becomes second nature.

---

## GRIT

---

As you've seen, controlling what you think is everything when it comes to staying in the game of rescuing your dreams. It's the mental strength that allows you to climb out of the pit, even when the weight of setbacks feels crushing.

That's what resilience is: your ability to rise again.

But grit?

Grit is what keeps you moving forward, step by step, with passion and perseverance—no matter how long the road or how steep the challenge. It's about locking in on your purpose, refusing to quit, and keeping your eyes on the prize.

And when your purpose is strong enough, you won't want to look at anything else.

When you combine the ability to rise with the determination to keep going, you create an unstoppable force—something that's resolute.

Your grit requires your resilience. Because if you can't get back up and rise, how will you ever keep move forward?

But grit doesn't just demand resilience. It demands focus—a disciplined ability to zero in on what's within your control and release everything else outside of it. Because while the journey to rescue your dreams will always come with uncertainties, your power lies in how you prepare and where you direct your energy.

## The Dichotomy of Control

Imagine an archer deep in the woods.

Their target, a deer grazing in the clearing ahead, is more than just sport—it's survival. The archer's stomach growls with hunger, and their heart pounds with the pressure of the shot.

The stakes couldn't be higher. And missing isn't an option.

But the archer knows better than to obsess over the outcome. Once the arrow is released, so many things could happen. A gust of wind might throw it off course. The deer could move. A branch might fall, knocking the arrow in flight. These are things beyond their control.

So, the archer focuses entirely on what they can control.

They examine their arrows, selecting the straightest one. Fingers glide along the quills, ensuring they're perfectly intact to keep the arrow steady in flight. They test the bowstring's tension, ensuring it's taut enough to send the arrow with force and precision. Nocking the arrow, they find their footing, steady their breathing, and align their sight with the target.

The moment comes.

The string is drawn back.

Their focus sharpens.

They exhale—and release.

The arrow flies ...

And more often than not, the arrow finds its mark.

It's the same with your efforts. You can't control every outcome, but you can control your preparation, your focus, and the energy you bring to the table. With each attempt, you refine your aim, sharpen your skills, and grow more capable.

When you focus on what you can control—your mindset, your consistency, and your systems—you'll hit more targets than you miss. And the more deliberate your efforts, the better those efforts will be.

### Hope Is Not a Strategy

Throughout that moment, the archer was full of hope. They hoped the arrow would strike its target, of course. But even more, they hoped that their experience—all the years spent honing their skills, every shot that missed and taught them something new—would pay off when it mattered most.

See, their hope wasn't in hope itself.

It was in themselves.

Hope is a powerful motivator. It gives you a reason to start and something to hold onto when the road gets tough. But hope alone isn't enough to get you where you want to go. Your hope needs to be fueled by consistent action and supported by tools, strategies, and systems.

Think about the tools you've built throughout this book: insights to strengthen your mindset, powerful questions to help you identify your needs, perimeters to create boundaries, courage to fly, and techniques to stay resilient.

You've learned how to clarify who you are, where you're going, and how to anchor yourself in purpose when things get hard.

With tools like these, your hope lies in you and your capabilities.

And you're not just equipped to meet your goals, but to surpass them—because you're capable of far more than you've ever imagined.

Most people don't dream big enough—not because their dreams aren't worthy, but because they don't fully believe they're capable of achieving them. Lacking the tools and purpose to sustain those dreams, they shrink them into something safe and predictable.

But what if you dared to go further?

Here's something to consider—most of us set goals we're confident we can achieve if we just do the work. Think about that: *if we just DO the work*, the goal is within reach. And yet, how many dreams remain buried simply because the work didn't get done?

So, what happens if you don't just set a goal, but a stretch goal?

A stretch goal dares you to move beyond what you think is possible. It pushes you to reach farther, grow more, and uncover strengths you didn't even know you had.

It's like setting out to catch the moon. A stretch goal tells you to aim for the stars. Even if you don't quite reach them, you'll catch the moon—and maybe even a few planets along the way.

And now knowing that the tools you've learned will help you go farther than ever, we have to make sure that your extra effort is focused on what matters most. Which brings us to two important questions that test your grit; what are you willing to do to make your dream a reality? And what are you willing to go through to achieve it?

Think of these questions as filters for your life. They help bring clarity to what truly matters.

Open up your journal and write the first question down:

**What are you willing to do to make your dream a reality?**

- Are you willing to save money, budget, or take on a second job?

- Are you ready to leave behind a relationship, draw boundaries, or pursue opportunities that feel risky or uncomfortable?

- Are you prepared to dedicate hours to practicing, learning, or refining your skills—even when progress feels slow?

This is about the things *you* choose to go through, knowing overcoming the obstacles is worth the payoff.

Think about tough decisions you've made in the past and what you were able to endure in order to have something that meant more to you than what you may have sacrificed, or how you may have been challenged.

Now answer the second question:

**What are you willing to go through to achieve it?**

- Are you willing to face rejection, criticism, or discomfort?

- Are you ready to endure self-doubt, frustration, or the fear that you're not good enough?

- Are you prepared to commit to long hours, early mornings, or sacrifices that demand more than you thought you had?

This is about the things that you *don't* choose, they're out of your control, the inevitable storms that could devastate what you've known, and they're coming to push you back to where you started.

Reflect back to times you pressed on, even though the rug was pulled out from under you, people tried to hold you back, or life struck you a blow when your guard was down. What was so important in those moments that you kept moving forward?

And while in the storm, did you believe you had the resolve to keep going?

These answers will reveal the foundation of your grit—what you're willing to fight for and what you refuse to give up on.

---

## ALL TOGETHER NOW

---

At the end of Chapter 9, you began to uncover your purpose—those moments when your life hummed with meaning and clarity. But we acknowledged then that the process wasn't complete.

Because you have to get clear not just about what makes you feel alive, strong, and impactful. You also have to know what is so important that you will pursue it till your last breath come hell or high water.

That's why this chapter exists: to help you see what's worth rising for and what's worth taking another step for, no matter what.

Reflect on the vision you started at the beginning of this book and refined in Chapter 4. That vision was your dream life—a life shaped by meaning, joy, and fulfillment.

**Ask yourself:**

- **Is the effort you're willing to give aligned with the life you want to create?**

- **Does that life make you feel alive, strong, and fulfilled?**

- **Does your dream life stretch beyond yourself and into meaningful impact with others?**

When you bring it all together—your dream life, the monsters you're willing to fight, the storms you're willing to endure, and the connections you want to create—you'll see your purpose with stunning clarity.

And now, it all comes full circle.

In Part 1, you laid the foundation by answering **Who are you?** That's the solid base that holds everything together—the unshakable truth of your identity.

In Part 2, you defined **Where are you going?** That became the structure you've been building, brick by brick, vision by vision, with every choice and action.

And now, it's time for the capstone—the final, defining piece that completes it all.

---

## WHY ARE YOU GOING THERE?

---

When people ask me why I do what I do—why I've spent years helping others bring the best of themselves to this world—I often hesitate for a moment. Not because I don't know the answer, but because it's so deeply rooted in who I am that even putting it into words feels like opening a door to my soul.

*Why am I going there?*

To help you rescue your dreams, so *you* can transform *your* reality.

Because I believe that every single person has a light within them—a force that can illuminate their world in ways no one else can.

My purpose has never been to tell you to become like me. It's to remind you that at your core, you are already enough. And to encourage you to rescue the unique brilliance only you can bring to the world.

For me, the answers to these questions have been the foundation of my journey:

- **Who Are You?**

   "I'm sunlight."

- **Where Are You Going?**

   "I *[I'm going to]* illuminate the dark corners of people's lives so they can see what's keeping them anchored in place—so they know what's been holding them back from the life they forgot they wanted to live."

- **Why Are You Going There?**

"To help you rescue your dreams, so you can transform your reality."

That's my identity. That's my vision. That's my purpose.

But this book isn't about *my* answers—it's about helping you find *yours*. And your answers will be unique to your journey.

So now, it's time to answer this final question for yourself.

Grab your journal.

On a fresh page, at the very top, write: **Why am I going there?**

Take a moment to reflect on everything you've uncovered in this book—your identity, your vision, your values, your goals. Let this question pull it all together.

Write it out. Let it flow. And don't worry about being clever with it. Don't overthink it either. Focus on what you simply can't stop yourself from doing no matter the odds, and how it positively impacts those around you.

Once you've written your answer, look at it closely. Ask yourself:

- **Does this feel true?**
- **How does this purpose align with the world I want to help create?**
- **Who else benefits when I step into this purpose?**

If the answer feels incomplete, take your time to revise it until it feels right. Try it on, take it for a spin, until it rolls off your tongue without cringing. There's no rush. This is your guiding purpose, and it deserves your care and attention.

When you've crafted your answer, go to the mirror. The one with all the reminders taped to it.

Say it out loud: **Why am I going there?**

Declare your answer boldly, unapologetically. Let it settle into your heart and mind.

Then guess what?

Take that sheet of paper, tear it out, and tape it next to the other pages you've written—**Who Are You?** and **Where Are You Going?**

Let these declarations remind you every day of the incredible journey you're on and the life *you're* creating. They're proof that you're living at full choice, being the person you were always meant to be, doing the work you were created to do, for a purpose only you can fulfill.

---

## SO NOW WHAT?

---

Now it's time to live—And to take another step.

And then another after that.

Because there's so much out there for you to experience, continue learning from, and grow through.

And your purpose is calling you ever upward.

So press on, keep rising, and keep going until your dreams are rescued—and your reality is transformed.

# THE END
# IS THE BEGINNING

Take a deep breath.

Not just a casual inhale, but a full, deep, I've-done-some-serious-work breath. The kind that expands your chest and settles into your bones. Because whether you realize it yet or not, you've just traveled through something big.

And now, we're back to where we started. **You are here.**

But this time, *here* is different.

Because now you know who you are, where you're going, and why you're going there.

At the beginning of this book, you took stock of your life—the reality you were standing in, the dreams you wanted to rescue, and the gap in between.

But as I mentioned, that first version might have still been tangled up in head trash, expectations, and comparison. It might have had traces of what others wanted for you, what seemed reasonable, or what felt safe.

Which is why in Part 2 you looked at it again—not to rewrite the dream, but to see it clearly. To strip away everything that wasn't truly yours. And as you've moved through this book, step by step, you've reinforced that what you want is worth fighting for.

And now, it's time to take a last look at the **You Are Here** exercise and see where you stand now.

**What has changed for you?**

My deepest hope is that a lot has changed for you. Or at least something significant has. That because of investing time and energy into yourself, you've become better for it.

And that means for some of you, this is a victory lap.

You've reclaimed something you lost, reconnected with a dream you forgot, or built something entirely new. Maybe you even fully saved the life you forgot you wanted.

And if so, the question becomes: **What's next?**

For others, you may still be in the process.

You've made progress, but there's still work to do. Which is okay because dreams don't always get rescued overnight. There's power in the long game, so keep at it and take heart.

Because of this book, and the work you've put in, you now have tools for life to make sure each step of your journey is heading in the right direction.

And those tools? They're not just for today, but for every challenge, decision, and dream ahead.

You've learned how to identify your limits, obstacles, and unmet needs. You know when you're running on empty. When something is missing. When your boundaries are being tested. When a challenge needs to be confronted instead of avoided.

Now you don't *just* recognize these things—you know what to do about them.

And just to ensure that you never get stuck again, let me show you something you may not have realized you were building all along—a framework for how to live.

I call it the recipe for a fulfilling life:

## 1. What do you want?

This is one of the greatest questions you can ask yourself in order to keep moving forward and to stay unstuck. And the great thing is, you know how to separate what *you* want from what the world expects of you.

## 2. What prevents you from having it?

In the past, you might have been unsure of this answer. But now, you already know how to uncover it—because of everything you learned in Part 2. You know how to identify unmet needs, obstacles, and patterns that might keep you anchored in place.

## 3. What are strong steps you can take?

You know these tools—backward planning, SMART goals, strategic action. You know how to bridge the gap between where you are and where you're going.

## 4. Who's going to help you?

That's your Connected worldview. You know that going it alone isn't strength—it's unnecessary struggle. And there are people out there who will support you on your journey.

This is a recipe that will serve you forever. Whenever you feel lost, ask yourself these four questions. They'll keep you moving, evolving, standing and delivering.

## So now what?

Well, if you've done the work, wrestled with the questions, and put in the reps—you don't just know more. You are more.

This journey has changed you.

And now?

Now, you have everything you need to rescue your dreams and transform your reality.

So, keep rising like the sun.

And go boldly, ever upward.

## ABOUT THE AUTHOR

Adam Mock, LCS is a gifted speaker, facilitator, and Leadership Coaching Specialist. Through his unique Rescue Your Dreams® approach, he helps individuals and organizations transform their realities and unlock their full potential.

With nearly 30 years of leadership experience, Adam serves as the Executive Director of Leadership Development for Triple Threat, facilitating team development trainings for global brands and Fortune 500 companies. He has led transformative experiences for diverse audiences worldwide, inspiring growth, resilience, and lasting change. He also works with Olympic gold medalists, Hall of Famers, and world champions, helping them transition beyond their athletic careers.

Trained and mentored by Dr. Doug McKinley, Adam specializes in principle-based leadership, dynamic communication, and emotional intelligence. Beyond the corporate world, he works with individuals looking to transform their lives—helping them step into their authentic selves, build confidence, and create a life filled with passion and purpose.

When he's not coaching, you can find him getting lost in music, mountain biking, or hiking in the woods.

For more visit: **adammock.com**
Instagram: **@adammock.lcs**